DK EYEW

TOP 10
SAN FRANCISCO

LOOK FOR!
___ Booklet ___ Blu-ray
___ Insert ___ CD
_7_ Maps ___ DVD
___ Disc

JEFFREY KENNEDY

W9-ANF-343

Top 10 San Francisco Highlights

The Top 10 of Everything

DK | Penguin Random House

CONTENTS

San Francisco Area by Area

Streetsmart

The information in this DK Eyewitness Top 10 Travel Guide is checked annually. Every effort has been made to ensure that this book is as up-to-date as possible at the time of going to press. Some details, however, such as telephone numbers, opening hours, prices, gallery hanging arrangements and travel information are liable to change. The publishers cannot accept responsibility for any consequences arising from the use of this book, nor for any material on third party websites, and cannot guarantee that any website address in this book will be a suitable source of travel information. We value the views and suggestions of our readers very highly. Please write to: Publisher, DK Eyewitness Travel Guides, Dorling Kindersley, 80 Strand, London WC2R 0RL, Great Britain, or email travelguides@dk.com.

Welcome to
San Francisco

The clacking wheels of cable cars. Steaming crab pots. Red and gold pagodas. Vibrant gay bars. Victorian mansions. The stunning bay, spanned by the glowing Golden Gate Bridge. And, always, fascinating people. This jewel of a city has something for all comers – and, with Eyewitness Top 10 San Francisco, it's yours to explore.

The misty hills of San Francisco have known Spanish conquistadors, Mexican settlers, the fortune seekers of the Gold Rush, and today's lively Latin American, European, Filipino, Russian, and Pan-Asian populations – each with their own festivals, neighborhoods, and eateries. Cultural diversity in this town is impossible to ignore – just walk down the street to hear a babble of languages. **North Beach** is home to Italians, the **Mission** is Hispanic and Asian, and **Chinatown** speaks for itself. The variety of ethnic restaurants is vast – there are over 3,500 places to eat in this foodie town: sushi bars, *taquerías*, dim sum parlors, brasseries, and Michelin-starred restaurants.

The city shines with culture, from the **San Francisco Museum of Modern Art** and the **de Young Museum** to opera in **Golden Gate Park** and the **Fillmore Street Jazz Festival**. To intrepid explorers, the city reveals her more hidden treasures, from the backstreet **Tin How Temple** to the cypress-tree sculptures in the **Presidio** forest. The city's annual events are legendary: the **Bay to Breakers** race, the explosive **Chinese New Year** parade, and of course the eyebrow-raising pageant of the **Pride Celebration Parade**.

Whether you're coming for a weekend or a week, our Top 10 guide brings together the best of everything the city has to offer, from iconic sights like **Alcatraz** to day trips to the **Wine Country**. It gives you tips throughout, from seeking out what's free to avoiding the crowds, plus easy-to-follow itineraries, planned to help you visit a clutch of sights in a short space of time. Add inspiring photography and detailed maps, and you've got the essential pocket-sized travel companion. **Enjoy the book, and enjoy San Francisco.**

Clockwise from top: **Golden Gate Bridge, statue at the Palace of Fine Arts, a cable car, sailing by Alcatraz, Golden Gate Park, Transamerica Pyramid, detail of City Hall's interior**

Exploring San Francisco

From the back alleys of Chinatown to the Pacific shores, San Francisco offers visitors everything from historic sites and museums to cruises in the vast bay. Here are some ideas for making the most of your stay, whether you have a weekend to fit in the "must sees," or have enough time for day trips and exploring the city's hidden gems.

Pagoda, Japanese Tea Garden

Ferry Building

Two Days in San Francisco

Day ❶
MORNING

Start the day at **Fisherman's Wharf** (see pp16–17) where the Eagle Café on the second floor of **Pier 39** (see p16) serves American breakfasts with Bay views. Then take the **Cable Car** to **Union Square** (see p89), where luxury department stores and boutiques glitter around the historic plaza.

AFTERNOON

Walk a few blocks to **Yerba Buena Gardens** (see pp32–3), a sprawling park and arts mecca. Highlights include **SFMOMA** (see pp30–31; reopening after renovations in 2016) and the state-of-the-art Cineplex at

Metreon (see p32). Just across the street is the **Contemporary Jewish Museum** (see p33). End the day with dinner in **Chinatown** (see pp22–3).

Day ❷
MORNING

After a Dungeness crab omelette and Irish coffee at **The Buena Vista Café** (see p101), take a ferry across the Bay to **Alcatraz** (see pp18–19) for a tour of the historic prison; the audio guide is a must.

AFTERNOON

Walk or bike across the **Golden Gate Bridge** (see pp12–13) and back, then ramble on the shoreline past **Crissy Field**, **Aquatic Park** (see p98), **Marina Green** (see p56), and the **Hyde Street Pier**, followed by a seafood feast at **Scoma's** (see p101).

Four Days in San Francisco

Day ❶
MORNING
In **Golden Gate Park** (see pp24–5), take tea in the **Japanese Tea Garden**. Nearby is the **de Young Museum** (see pp28–9). Enjoy lunch on the terrace of its sculpture garden.

AFTERNOON
Explore the rainforest and the living roof at the **California Academy of Sciences** (see pp26–7), row around **Stow Lake** (see p24), and admire the **Dutch Windmill** (see p24). Have dinner at **Cliff House** (see p123).

Day ❷
MORNING
Learn about early California history at the oldest building in the city, **Mission Dolores** (see pp34–5), before heading to a sidewalk table at **Caffè Trieste** (see p76) in North Beach for a pizza slice, focaccia sandwich, and a cappuccino. Up the street, the spires of **Saints Peter and Paul Church** (see p92) tower over Washington Square, while **Coit Tower** (see p92) has Depression-era murals.

AFTERNOON
Head to **Yerba Buena Gardens** (see pp32–3) and explore **SFMOMA** (see pp30–31; reopening after renovations in 2016) and the other museums, galleries, and gardens. Afterwards, walk to **Chinatown** (see pp22–3) and discover the **Tin How Temple** (see p62). Enjoy dim sum dumplings at Hang Ah Tea Room (1 Pagoda Place).

Day ❸
MORNING
Take in the woodlands, vistas, and Civil War sites of the **Presidio** (see p56). Savor a Mexican lunch at the impressive Officers' Club.
AFTERNOON
Explore **Fisherman's Wharf** (see pp16–17), being sure not to miss the sea lions at **Pier 39** (see p16). Then take a ferry across the Bay to **Alcatraz** (see pp18–19) for a tour of the prison. End the day with a ride in a **Cable Car** to **Union Square** (see p89) for dinner.

Day ❹
MORNING
Cross the **Golden Gate Bridge** (see pp12–13) and drive an hour north to the **Wine Country** (see pp36–9). Visit the **Hess Collection** (see p37) to enjoy a winery tour and tasting.
AFTERNOON
Enjoy the spas and eateries of **Yountville** (see p36) before returning to the city and **Nob Hill** (see p87) for cocktails at the **InterContinental Mark Hopkins** (see p145).

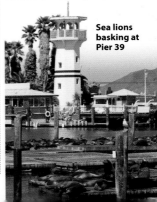

Sea lions basking at Pier 39

Key
━ Two-day itinerary
━ Four-day itinerary

Top 10 San Francisco Highlights

The roof of the California Academy of Sciences, Golden Gate Park

TOP 10 San Francisco's Highlights

Most visitors, after a few days of taking in the sights and sounds of San Francisco, will likely tell you it's their favorite city. The geographical setting evokes so much drama, the light seems clearer, the colors more vivid, the cultural diversity so captivating and inviting, that it's a place almost everyone can fall in love with at first sight.

Golden Gate Bridge 1
This symbol of the city is one of the world's largest single span bridges *(see pp12–13)*.

2 Cable Cars
These little troopers now form the world's only system of its kind that still plays a daily role in urban life *(see pp14–15)*.

3 Fisherman's Wharf
The views from here are unmatched. You can also see sea lions and try great seafood *(see pp16–17)*.

Alcatraz 4
"The Rock" continues to capture the imagination. The views from the ferry are among the best parts of a visit *(see pp18–21)*.

Chinatown 5
The exotic feel of one of the world's largest Chinese communities outside of Asia makes this a magnet for locals and visitors alike *(see pp22–3)*.

Golden Gate Park ⑥

The city boasts one of the world's largest public parks, with natural beauty and fine museums *(see pp24–7)*.

⑧ SFMOMA

San Francisco's architectural landmark houses 20th-century masterworks of painting, sculpture and photography, digital installations, and temporary exhibitions *(see pp30–31)*.

⑦ de Young Museum

A cultural landmark housing American, Oceanian, and African art, as well as temporary exhibits *(see pp28–9)*.

⑨ Mission Dolores

The city's oldest building is also the only intact chapel among the 21 missions Father Junípero Serra founded. Its founding days before the Declaration of Independence makes the city older than the US *(see pp34–5)*.

⑩ The Wine Country

French, Italian, and Spanish winemakers have now also established vineyards here. Not to be missed *(see pp36–9)*.

TOP 10 ★ Golden Gate Bridge

As with most of the world's wonders, many said the Golden Gate Bridge could never be built – the span was too wide, the ocean too deep, and the cost too great. In 1872, railroad tycoon Charles Crocker conceived the idea, but it took a visionary engineer, Joseph Strauss, to put forth a realistic proposal in 1921. After 10 years of opposition, funding was finally secured. The bridge opened in 1937, and has been an emblem of San Francisco, and America's icon on the Pacific, ever since.

Deco Style ①
The bridge (right) owes its striking style to the consulting architect Irving F. Morrow. He simplified the pedestrian railings to uniform posts placed far enough apart to allow for unobstructed, breathtaking views.

② **Bridge Celebrations**
The bridge opened on May 27, 1937, with some 200,000 pedestrians. Fifty years later, the ritual was repeated. On May 27, 2012, the 75th anniversary of the opening was marked.

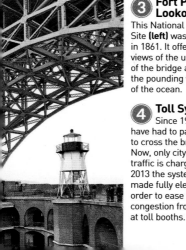

③ **Fort Point Lookout**
This National Historic Site (left) was completed in 1861. It offers soaring views of the underside of the bridge and of the pounding waters of the ocean.

④ **Toll System**
Since 1937, cars have had to pay a toll to cross the bridge. Now, only city-bound traffic is charged, and in 2013 the system was made fully electronic in order to ease the traffic congestion from stopping at toll booths.

⑤ **Maintenance**
Repairing and painting the bridge (below) is an ongoing task. The paint protects it from the high salt content in the air, which corrodes the steel components.

THE STATISTICS
The length of the steel wires used to make the cables of the bridge is enough to circle the earth three times. It is also brilliantly "over-engineered" and is said to be five times stronger than it needs to be to withstand the winds and tides it endures daily. At the time it was built, it was the longest suspension bridge in the world (it now ranks ninth) and took just over four years to build. About 40 million vehicles cross the bridge annually, streaming across six lanes of traffic, along its 1.7-mile (2.7-km) length. The bridge is equipped with two foghorns, each with a different pitch, and 360-degree flashing red beacons. The bridge has been closed due to high winds only three times in its history.

(8) Building the Bridge

Strauss introduced the use of hard hats **(above)** and a safety net that saved 19 workers' lives.

(9) Hiking and Biking

Every visitor should walk or cycle across at least part of the bridge.

(10) Marin Vista Point

Crossing from the side, pull off just before the end to take in the startling panorama from the Vista Point and look back at the hills and spires of the city.

Star Turns in Movies (6)

The bridge has starred in many movies, most notably Alfred Hitchcock's *Vertigo*, in which James Stewart pulls Kim Novak from the raging surf, just east of Fort Point *(see p98)*. In *A View to a Kill* **(right)**, 007 and Christopher Walken battle it out, both clinging to its aerial heights.

(7) Protective Barriers

The Golden Gate Bridge is the number-one spot in the world for suicides. As yet there have been no barriers effective enough to prevent this, but there are bars in place for general safety.

NEED TO KNOW

MAP C1 ▪
▪ (415) 921-5858
▪ www.goldengate.org

Cruises operate Mar–Oct

▪ **For a uniquely powerful view of the bridge while enjoying a Sunday champagne brunch, opt for one of the many cruises on the Bay, departing from the Embarcadero Pier and Sausalito. Quality purveyors are Hornblower Cruises ((415) 438-8300, www. hornblower.com), and Call of the Sea/Seaward ((415) 331-3214, www. callofthesea.org).**

🔟⭐ Cable Cars

It's impossible not to love these vestiges of another age, as they valiantly make their way up the precipitous hills. Yet they came perilously close to being scrapped in 1947, when a "progressive" mayor announced it was time for buses to take their place. An outraged citizenry prevailed, and the system was declared a National Historic Landmark in 1964. In the early 1980s, it underwent a $60 million overhaul. The present service of about 40 cars covers some 10 miles (16 km).

1 Bell
While operating up and down the hills, the cable car's bell **(right)** is used by the grip person like a klaxon, to warn other vehicles and pedestrians of imminent stops, starts, and turns.

2 Grip Person
The grip person **(below)** must be quick-thinking and strong to operate the heavy gripping levers and braking mechanisms. The grip is like a huge pair of pliers that clamps onto the cable to pull the car along.

3 Cars
Cable cars **(right)** come in two types: one that has a turnaround system, one that does not. All of them are numbered, have wood-and-brass fittings in the 19th-century style, and are often painted in differing colors.

4 Conductor
Collects fares, but also makes sure that everyone travels safely, and that the grip person has room to work.

5 Braking
Wheel brakes press against the wheels; track brakes press against the tracks when the grip person pulls a lever; the emergency brake is a steel wedge forced into the rail slot.

6 Riding Styles
There is a choice of sitting inside a glassed-in compartment, sitting outside on wooden benches, or hanging onto poles and standing on the running board. The third option is the best one for enjoying the enticing sights, sounds, and smells of San Francisco.

CABLE CARS AND STREETCARS

Andrew Hallidie's cable car system dates from August 2, 1873, when he tested his prototype based on mining cars. It was an immediate success and spawned imitators in more than a dozen cities worldwide. However, 20 years later, it was set to be replaced by the electric streetcar. Fortunately, resistance to above-ground wires, corruption in City Hall, and finally the 1906 earthquake, sidetracked those plans. The cable car was kept for the steepest lines, while the streetcar took over the longer, flatter routes.

8 Turntables
Part of the fun of the cable car experience is being there to watch when the grip person and conductor turn their car around for the return trip **(left)**. The best view is at Powell and Market Streets.

9 Cable Car Museum
Downstairs, look at the giant sheaves (wheels), which keep the cables moving throughout the system **(above)**; upstairs there are displays of some of the earliest cable cars.

10 Routes
The three existing routes cover the Financial District, Nob Hill **(below)**, Chinatown, North Beach, Russian Hill, and Fisherman's Wharf areas. As these are always important destinations for visitors – and for many residents, too – most people will find that a cable car ride is a practical as well as a pleasurable experience.

7 Cables
The underground cables are 1.25 inches (3 cm) in diameter and consist of six steel strands of 19 wires, wrapped around a shock-absorbing rope.

NEED TO KNOW

MAP M3

Cable Car Museum: 1201 Mason St at Washington ▪ (415) 474-1887 ▪ www. cablecarmuseum.org

Open Apr–Sep: 10am–6pm daily; Oct–Mar: 10am–5pm daily

▪ Rather than wait in the long lines at a cable car terminus, do what the locals do and walk up a stop or two, where you can hop on right away for a $6 fee – then hold on!

▪ The $6 fare is for one ride, in one direction, with no transfers. Consider getting a CityPass or a Muni Passport for one day ($17) or longer (see p134).

TOP 10 ⭐ Fisherman's Wharf

Tourists enjoying takeout crab cocktails and sourdough bread crowd the sidewalks and souvenir stands of the old seaside wharf district. Amid today's seafood eateries, aquarium, wax museum, and bay cruise piers, fishing boats become great photo ops as their catches of Dungeness crab and Pacific fish are unloaded. Rowdy old days of the 1850s are reenacted on masted schooners, while a World War II-era submarine and a Liberty ship recall the city's long history as a major port.

PIER 39 ①
One of the most popular attractions **(right)**, set on a landscaped pier with dazzling bay views, two levels of dining, live entertainment, and tourist-oriented shops. Get discount coupons at the California Welcome Center. Families love the bungee jump, mirror maze, games arcade, and carousel.

② Ghirardelli Square
The Ghirardelli family used this square as the headquarters of the Ghirardelli Chocolate Company from 1859 until 1962. The site is now home to upscale shops and eateries *(see p100)*.

⑤ Boudin Bakery
This is the home of the famous chain of San Francisco sourdough breadmakers **(left)**. Try the crusty round loaf, best enjoyed warm from the oven with plenty of butter.

⑥ Madame Tussauds
Incredibly lifelike wax figures of movie stars, music legends, political and sports icons, and San Francisco celebrities are on display here. A scary "Dungeon" theatrical show is for ages 10 and up.

③ Aquarium of the Bay
The transparent tunnel of the aquarium visually immerses you in the San Francisco Bay marine habitat, where thousands of members of diverse ocean fauna disport themselves before your eyes. Video presentations and marine specialist guides help you to understand what you're seeing.

Anchorage Square ④ Shopping Center
In the heart of Fisherman's Wharf, with plenty of stores, restaurants, and entertainment **(right)**.

**Map of
Fisherman's Wharf**

7 The Cannery
Built as a warehouse in 1907, the building underwent a makeover in 1967, and it's now the site of some appealing boutiques, as well as tourist shops.

8 Fish Alley
This alley is possibly the last vestige of the authentic, workaday wharf. Here you can see fishing boats come in and watch as the catch of the day is landed and prepared for market.

9 Maritime National Historical Park
At the Hyde Street Pier (below) are vessels ranging from 1880s schooners and a spectacular 1886 square-rigger to 1900s tugs and the USS *Pampanito* World War II submarine.

10 SS Jeremiah O'Brien Liberty Ship
At Pier 45 floats this fully restored World War II Liberty ship. Take a free tour to hear tales of the thousands of troops ferried across the seas.

THE PORT OF SAN FRANCISCO
Born of the California Gold Rush of 1849, the Port of San Francisco (below) stretches nearly 8 miles (13 km) from the Hyde Street Pier to India Basin. A new cruise ship terminal hosts 80 cruise ship calls and 200,000 passengers annually, while freighters lumber under the Golden Gate Bridge and ferries, water taxis, fishing boats, and yachts bustle to and from the Ferry Building, Fisherman's Wharf, and Embarcadero piers and marinas.

NEED TO KNOW
MAP J3

Anchorage Sq Shopping Center: 2800 Leavenworth St ▪ (415) 775-6000

Aquarium of the Bay: Embarcadero ▪ (415) 623-5300

Open 9am–8pm daily (winter: 10am–6pm Mon–Thu, 10am–7pm Fri–Sun)

Adm $12–$20

Madame Tussauds: 145 Jefferson St ▪ (866) 223-4240 ▪ www.madame tussauds.com

Open 10am–8pm Sun–Thu, 10am–9pm Fri–Sat

Adm $16–$26

Maritime National Historical Park: 499 Jefferson St ▪ maritime.org

Open 9:30am–5pm daily

Adm $5; under-16s free

SS Jeremiah O'Brien Liberty Ship: Pier 45 ▪ (415) 544-0100 ▪ www. ssjeremiahobrien.org

Open 9am–4pm daily

Adm $6–$12; under-5s free

▪ For seafood, try one of the Wharf's oldest institutions, Scoma's (Pier 47 & Al Scoma Way; (415) 771-4383).

TOP 10 ⭐ Alcatraz

To the inmates physically confined on this island prison, their punishment was also psychological. They were in the midst of one of America's busiest harbors, and could probably hear the ceaseless procession of cars crossing the bridges and honking their horns. They could certainly see the ocean liners gliding to faraway ports – all reminders that life was near, but freedom very far.

THE HISTORY OF "THE ROCK"

The name "Alcatraz" derives from the Spanish *alcatraces*, for the birds that Spanish explorer Juan Manuel de Ayala observed here when he sailed into the Bay in 1775. In 1850, the island was set aside for the US Army to build a citadel, but defense became less of a priority and, in 1909, it became a military prison. In 1933 the Federal Government opened a maximum-security penitentiary here. Yet Alcatraz was not the "Devil's Island" that many think it was – the conditions were better than other prisons.

1 Chapel
Above the guardhouse, a Mission-style military chapel **(above)** was built in the 1920s. It was also used as living quarters and a school. During the post-1930s prison phase, it was used to house prison staff.

2 D Block
Prisoners who broke the strict rules were sent here for solitary confinement and kept in total darkness.

3 Exercise Yard
Good behavior qualified prisoners for a turn around the walled-in exercise yard **(left)**. Here, they could walk outside of their cells, where they spent between 16 and 23 hours a day.

4 Lighthouse
Alcatraz was the site of the first lighthouse built on the West Coast in 1854. The original was replaced in 1909 to tower above the new cell block **(above)**.

5 Control Room
From this bunker-like facility **(above)**, the guards controlled the security system. Next to the Control Room was the visiting area, where thick glass separated prisoners and visitors, and conversations were held over telephones.

6 Broadway
The corridor that separates C and B blocks was jokingly nicknamed by prisoners after New York City's glittering thoroughfare, famous for its nightlife. The intersection at the end was named "Times Square."

7 Cell Blocks
The cell house contains four free-standing cell blocks **(below)**. The complex was built by military prisoners in 1911 and was once the largest reinforced concrete building in the world. In all, there were 390 cells, but the prison population averaged only about 260 at any one time.

8 Warden's House
Until the house burned down in 1970, the warden's home **(below)** looked out to freedom. Designed in Mission Revival style, the home had 17 large rooms, and sweeping views of the Golden Gate Bridge and San Francisco's lights.

NEED TO KNOW

Alcatraz Cruises (Hornblower) from Pier 33: (415) 981-7625 (tickets and schedules) ▪ www.alcatrazcruises.com

Open daily

Adm: day tours – $30 adult, $28.25 senior, $18.25 child 5–11 years; night tours – $37 adult, $34.25 senior, $21.75 child 5–11 years; family packages available

Tour compulsory

▪ Picnicking is allowed on the dock, but you'll have to bring your own food.

▪ The weather is often blustery and cold on the island, and the trails and walkways rough. Wear warm clothes and strong, comfortable shoes.

▪ A cell-house audio tour explores the prison and its stories. It is available in eight languages and is included in the price of the ticket, as is the excellent ranger-guided tour.

---

9 Mess Hall
Meals were one of the few things prisoners had to look forward to, and they were generally well fed to quell rebellion. Note the sample menu at the entrance to the kitchen **(below)**.

10 Building 64
The theater and orientation center are located in the old barracks building behind the ferry jetty. The building also houses a bookstore, exhibits, and a multimedia show providing a historical overview of Alcatraz.

Stories from The Rock

Burt Lancaster in *Birdman of Alcatraz*

1 Robert "Birdman" Stroud

The most famous inmate was dubbed the "Birdman of Alcatraz," despite the fact that he was not permitted to conduct his avian studies during his 17 years here. Due to his violent nature, Stroud spent most of those years in solitary.

2 Birdman of Alcatraz

This 1962 movie presented Robert Stroud as a nature-loving ornithologist, bending historical fact to the service of a good story.

3 Al Capone

In 1934 Capone was among the first "official" shipment of prisoners. The infamous gangster was assigned menial jobs and treated like every other inmate.

4 George "Machine Gun" Kelly

Jailed in 1933 for kidnapping, Kelly was given a life sentence, and was sent to Alcatraz for 17 years of his sentence. He was considered a model prisoner by the officers.

5 Alvin "Creepy" Karpis

Karpis robbed his way through the Midwest between 1931 and 1936, and earned himself the title Public Enemy Number One. He was imprisoned on Alcatraz from 1936 to 1962. He committed suicide in 1979.

6 Morton Sobell

Charged with conspiracy to commit treason by spying for the Soviets, Sobell arrived on Alcatraz in 1952 and spent five years as its most famous political prisoner, being a victim of J. Edgar Hoover's witch hunt for Communist subversives. Once freed, Sobell returned to live in San Francisco for many years.

7 Anglin Brothers

The brothers, John and Clarence, are notable as two of the five known inmates to successfully escape from The Rock.

Clint Eastwood in *Escape from Alcatraz*

8 Escape from Alcatraz

Starring Clint Eastwood as Frank Morris, who escaped along with the Anglin brothers. Again, this 1979 film is largely Hollywood fiction. However, the depiction of prison life is reportedly accurate.

9 Frank Wathernam

The last prisoner to leave Alcatraz, on March 21, 1963.

10 The Rock

Hollywood has never lost its fascination with Alcatraz, as can be seen in this 1996 action thriller, starring Sean Connery.

NATIVE AMERICAN OCCUPATION

In 1969 Richard Oakes and 90 other Native Americans landed on Alcatraz, set up camp, and demanded that the government sell them the island for $24 worth of beads and red cloth. They claimed that this was the price their people had been paid in exchange for an island similar in size nearly 300 years earlier. The government considered forcibly removing the occupiers, but growing public support for the Native Americans forced officials to renew negotiations. However, in January, 1970, while playing on the rooftop of one of the buildings, Oakes' youngest daughter slipped and fell to her death; distraught, he and his family decided to abandon their claim. Sixty Native Americans remained, but as the stalemate dragged on, the majority slowly began to leave – only 15 chose to stay. In June, 1970, fires ravaged the warden's house, the recreation hall, the officers' club, and the lighthouse. Following this devastation, government troops staged a pre-dawn raid. The remaining Native Americans were arrested and the 19-month occupation came to an end.

John Anglin, escaped June, 1962

TOP 10
ESCAPE ATTEMPTS

1 December, 1937: Theodore Cole and Ralph Roe

2 May, 1938: Thomas Limerick, James Lucas, and Rufus Franklin

3 January, 1939: Arthur "Doc" Barker, Dale Stamphill, William Martin, Henry Young, and Rufus McCain

4 May, 1941: Joseph Cretzer, Sam Shockley, Arnold Kyle, and Lloyd Barkdoll

5 April, 1943: James Boarman, Harold Brest, Floyd Hamilton, and Fred Hunter

6 July, 1945: John Giles

7 May, 1946: Bernard Coy, Joseph Cretzer, Marvin Hubbard, Sam Shockley, Miran Thompson, and Clarence Carnes

8 September, 1958: Aaron Burgett and Clyde Johnson

9 June, 1962: Frank Morris and John and Clarence Anglin

10 December, 1962: John Paul Scott and Darl Parker

Native American in full ceremonial attire as he stands in an open prison cell in the former Alcatraz Prison during the Native American occupation.

Chinatown

This teeming, densely populated neighborhood, with its bright facades, noisy markets, exotic temples, and ethnic restaurants and shops, is like a city within the city – and a place every visit to San Francisco must include. The atmosphere recalls a typical southern Chinese town, although the architecture, customs, and public celebrations are distinctly American hybrids on a Cantonese theme. Overlook the tourist tackiness, check out some of the side alleys, and give yourself time to take it all in.

Chinatown Gate ①
A gift from Taiwan in 1970, this triple-pagoda southern entrance to Chinatown **(right)** was inspired by traditional Chinese village gates.

② Golden Gate Fortune Cookie Company
Fortune cookies were invented in San Francisco. Stop by to watch how the skilful workers slip the fortune message in the cookie mixture then fold it into the traditional shapes.

③ Chinese Six Companies
This building's brilliant facade is one of the most ornate in Chinatown. The Six Companies association was formed in 1882 to promote Chinese interests within the community.

④ Portsmouth Square
This was San Francisco's original town square – here, on July 9, 1846, the US flag was first raised when the port was seized from Mexico. Locals now use the area for tai chi and games of mah-jongg **(below)**.

⑤ St. Mary's Square
This square is graced by a stainless-steel and rose-granite statue of Sun Yat-sen by San Francisco sculptor Beniamino Bufano.

⑥ Chinese Historical Society of America
This building, designed by architect Julia Morgan in 1932, is the home of a learning center and a museum containing a 15,000-piece collection of artifacts, documents, photographs, and replicas that illustrate and explain the Chinese-American experience.

7 Stockton Street Chinese Markets

At these authentic markets **(left)** selling fresh produce, the real smells, sights, and sounds of Chinatown come into sharp focus.

8 Old Chinese Telephone Exchange

This three-tiered pagoda is now the East West Bank, and is the most distinctive work of architectural chinoiserie in Chinatown. It served as the telephone exchange up until the 1950s.

9 Chinese Culture Center

The Chinese Culture Center comprises an art gallery and a small crafts shop, which features the work of Chinese and Chinese-American artists.

10 Temples

There are a number of temples that incorporate Confucian, Taoist, and Buddhist elements. The Tin How Temple **(right)**, founded in 1852, is dedicated to the Queen of Heaven.

GOLD RUSH CANTONESE

Chinese immigrants began to arrive with the Gold Rush, to get rich quick and return home heroes. As it happened, things turned politically sour in China at the time, and many Chinese people stayed in the new land. There was, however, a racist backlash against them, resulting in the Chinese Exclusion Act of 1882, and Chinatown became a kind of ghetto, full of opium dens and vice. The act was repealed in 1943, and things have steadily improved ever since.

NEED TO KNOW

MAP N4

Chinese Culture Center: **MAP M5** ▪ Hilton Hotel, 750 Kearny St, 3rd floor ▪ (415) 986-1822 ▪ www.c-c-c.org

Chinese Historical Society of America: **MAP N5** ▪ 965 Clay St ▪ (415) 391-1188 ▪ www.chsa.org

Chinese Six Companies: **MAP N4** ▪ 843 Stockton St

Golden Gate Fortune Cookie Company: **MAP M4** ▪ 56 Ross Alley ▪ (415) 781-3956

Old Chinese Telephone Exchange: **MAP M4** ▪ 743 Washington St

Tin How Temple: **MAP N4** ▪ 125 Waverly Place, top floor

▪ Don't drive into Chinatown: it's very congested, and it can be impossible to find parking. Take the cable car instead – all three of the lines will get you there *(see p15)*.

▪ One of the most popular Chinese restaurants in San Francisco, Yank Sing, can be found here *(see p95)*.

TOP 10 ⭐ Golden Gate Park

This is every San Franciscan's beloved backyard. Weekends find hundreds of people here playing or relaxing. Almost every sort of recreational activity is available, from hiking to fishing. There's also the very first children's playground in the US, with the magnificent Herschel-Spillman Carousel, built in 1912 *(see p67)*. Even on a rainy day, the park offers world-class activities in the form of de Young Museum, the California Academy of Sciences, and Morrison Planetarium *(see pp26–7)*.

1 de Young Museum
Landmark museum showing art from Africa, America, and the Pacific, plus photographs and textiles *(see pp28–9)*.

2 Stow Lake and Strawberry Hill
Strawberry Hill is the island in the middle of this lake. Don't miss the Chinese moon-viewing pavilion on the island's eastern shore.

3 Victorian Conservatory of Flowers
The park's oldest building, a copy of one in London's Kew Gardens, shelters over 20,000 rare and exotic plants.

4 Japanese Tea Garden
This delightful garden is full of bonsai trees, rock gardens, exotic plantings, and pagodas **(right)**.

5 Buffalo Paddock
In 1984 a small herd of buffalo was given a home roaming under the eucalyptus trees.

6 Strybing Arboretum and Botanical Garden
More than 7,000 species live in areas including a Redwood Trail, an Ancient Plant Garden, and a Garden of Fragrance.

7 Giant Tree Fern Grove and John McLaren Rhododendron Dell
Coming upon the Giant Tree Fern Grove, with its huge, curling proto-flora gathered around a small lagoon, is like entering a primeval forest. The Rhododendron Dell contains the largest variety (850) of these blooms in any US garden.

8 Dutch Windmill and Queen Wilhelmina Tulip Garden
The windmill and the tulip garden that surrounds it **(left)** were both gifts from the queen of the Netherlands in 1902. The windmill is one of the world's largest and was restored in 1981.

NEED TO KNOW

MAP D4 ▪ Entrances on Fulton St, Lincoln Way, Stanyan St & the Great Hwy ▪ (415) 831-2700 ▪ www.sfrecpark.org

Open sunrise–sunset

California Academy of Sciences: Music Concourse ▪ www.calacademy.org

Open 9:30am–5pm Mon–Sat, 11am–5pm Sun

Adm $25–$35

Japanese Tea Garden: Hagiwara Tea Garden Drive

Open 9am–6pm

Adm $8 adult, $6 youth, $2 child/senior

Strybing Arboretum and Botanical Gardens: 9th Ave

Open Apr–Oct: 9am–6pm; Nov–Mar: 10am–5pm

▪ For information on and a map of the Golden Gate Park, stop off at the McLaren Lodge Visitor Center, which was originally the home of the park's chief gardener (501 Stanyan St, open 8:30am–5pm Mon–Fri).

🔟 Shakespeare Garden

This charming English garden **(above)** features the 200-odd flowers and herbs mentioned in the Bard's works. Bronze plaques quote the relevant passages.

Music Concourse ⑨

This area **(right)** hosts free concerts on Sundays and events by the San Francisco Opera *(see p68)*.

A MIRACLE OF LAND RECLAMATION

The park's more than 1,000 acres (405 ha) are some 3 miles (5 km) long and half a mile (1 km) wide, making it the largest cultivated urban park in the US. There are 27 miles (43 km) of footpaths, winding through lakes, gardens, waterfalls, and forests. But it was not always so. Before the 1870s the entire area was sandy wastes and scrubland. William Hammond Hall made great progress over two decades, then hired Scottish gardener John McLaren in 1890. "Uncle John," as he was known, made the park his life's work, devoting himself to its perfection until his death in 1943, aged 97.

California Academy of Sciences

1 Morrison Planetarium

Fly through space and time to the very limits of the known universe, and gain a new perspective on the planet we call home, with high-tech exhibits and technology, including an all-digital dome **(above)**. Shows are presented daily.

2 Coral Reef

This is one of the deepest living coral reef displays in the world, exhibiting a range of aquatic life from the reefs and mangroves of the Philippines. Sharks and rays can be seen from the surface, while the coral, reef fish, and colorful clams **(below)** can be viewed close up through underwater windows.

3 Discovery Tidepool

Stroke a starfish, get cozy with some hermit crabs, or pick up a sea slug in this hands-on, hands-wet attraction, which is part of the California Coast exhibits. Here, you don't have to worry about slippery rocks to get close to these coastal creatures. The pool is staffed by helpful volunteers who will tell you what you're handling and keep the animals safe, too.

4 Penguin Feeding Time

The colony of black-footed penguins located in African Hall are fed twice daily, and it's always a spectacle enjoyed by the whole family. Penguins may waddle on land, but their grace is evident when you observe them dive and glide effortlessly through the water to catch their meal.

5 California Coast

Explore habitats ranging from salt marshes to turbulent rocky inlets and meet a variety of native fish and invertebrates. The main tank – an exhibit featuring the marine habitats of the Gulf of the Farallones National Marine Sanctuary – is 100,000 gallons in capacity, with large viewing windows, and a crashing wave surge system.

6 Rainforests

Visitors can experience four rainforest environments in an enormous glass dome: the Amazonian Flooded Forest, the Borneo Forest

7 Water Planet
Dozens of tanks and a range of interactive media are used to inform all ages of what it takes to survive under water. A variety of fish, including jellyfish and the strange-looking paddlefish, reptiles like zebra morays, amphibians, and insects are on display.

8 The Swamp
Part of the Steinhart Aquarium, which holds about 38,000 animals from around the world, the Swamp is home to alligator snapping turtles, Claude (the famous albino alligator), and exhibits on frogs, rattlesnakes, and salamanders.

9 Living Roof
The museum is topped with a 2.5-acre (1-ha) living roof, which is planted with over 1.7 million native Californian plants. Take an elevator up to the rooftop deck to enjoy the views and learn about the benefits of sustainable architecture.

10 African Hall
Magnificent dioramas display a range of African fauna in their natural surroundings, such as the straight-horned oryx, gorillas, antelope (below), and cheetahs. The human evolution exhibit tracks the fascinating history of our species with fossils of our early ancestors. A colony of busy African penguins, which is viewed through a vast window, ends the exhibit.

Floor, the Madagascar Rainforest Understory, and the Costa Rica Rainforest Canopy. They include hundreds of tropical plants (above) and a range of creatures: piranhas, flying lizards, parrots, and chameleons.

TOP10 ⭐ de Young Museum

The immense copper-clad de Young Museum looms as a cultural and architectural landmark above a canopy of plane trees in the Music Concourse of the Golden Gate Park. It is a bastion of American, Oceanian, and African art, as well as housing a world-famous textile collection. The de Young also lures crowds to blockbuster temporary exhibits such as King Tut's tomb, colossal Olmec stone heads, the gems of Bulgari, works by Henri Matisse, and Impressionist masterpieces.

3 Photography
Spanning the history of the medium, the de Young is strong on 19th-century American and European images, from documentation of the 1894 California Midwinter International Exposition and daguerreotypes to early and contemporary San Franciscan scenes.

de Young Museum

1 Textiles and Costumes
Three centuries of fiber art and fashion include bark cloth, Central Asian and North Indian silks, the most important Anatolian kilims outside Turkey **(above)**, European tapestries, and early 20th-century couture.

2 Hamon Observation Tower
It's free to ascend the 144-ft (43.8-m) tower to the 360-degree glass-walled observation deck **(below)** for treetop views of the Music Concourse, the park, the city, and beyond to the Golden Gate Bridge and the Marin Headlands.

4 Museum Gardens
Don't miss the remnants of the California Mid-winter International Exposition of 1894 in the surrounding shady walking trails: the Pool of Enchantment, the vases, and the sphinxes **(right)**.

5 20th-Century American and Bay Area Artists
Georgia O'Keeffe's *Petunias* is among the contemporary master-works on display in the museum, while Chiura Obata, Richard Diebenkorn, Wayne Thiebaud, and sculptors Ruth Asawa and Robert Arneson are among the local icons featured.

6 Temporary Exhibits
Wildly popular and requiring advance tickets, a variety of temporary exhibitions have included ancient glass from the Holy Land, Jean Paul Gaultier fashion, and many more.

7 Artful Kids
The de Young welcomes kids to free Saturday art classes, summer camps, and a monthly artist-in-residence workshop for the whole family. Guided tours for families are followed by studio workshops taught by professional artists.

8 American Collection

Founded by donations from the Rockefellers, this comprehensive collection, from 1670 to the present, has more than 3,000 decorative arts objects, 800 sculptures, and 1,000 paintings, including *Boatmen on the Missouri* by George Caleb Bingham **(left)**.

A DAY AT THE DE YOUNG

Take breaks from total art immersion by enjoying the indoor-outdoor café and the rambling sculpture garden (you can come in and out of the museum all day with your ticket). Audio and docent-led tours enrich the experience, as do curator talks and workshops. Art enthusiasts flock to the "Friday Nights at the de Young" events of music, panels, and interaction with artists, during which cocktails are served. The two-level store is stocked with art books, exhibit programs, logo items, and signature jewelry, textiles, posters, and prints relating to the exhibits. Kids can hang out in the toy- and book-filled children's section.

9 Art of the Americas

Pre-Columbian and ancient Native American artifacts are displayed in these galleries, including a stunning group of Teotihuacan murals. The Weisel Family Collection spans 1,000 years of Native American objects and textiles.

10 Africa and the Pacific

Micronesian and Maori carvings, basketry, and over 1,400 pieces from across the regions are on view **(below)**, along with Scheller's collection of Masterworks of African Figurative Sculpture, depicting 140 ethnic groups.

NEED TO KNOW

MAP C4 ▪ 50 Hagiwara Tea Garden Drive, Golden Gate Park ▪ (415) 750-3600 ▪ www.famsf.org

Open 9:30am–5:15pm Tue–Sun; Apr–Nov: 9:30am–8:45pm Fri

The de Young is accessible via Muni lines 5, 44, and the N-Judah. Save $2 on admission with proof of public transit. Self-parking is available under the museum.

Adm $10 adult, $7 senior, $6 student/youth, free child 0–12 years; free first Tue of month; limited-run exhibitions may require separate tickets purchased in advance

Children are welcome, although baby backpacks and large bags are forbidden, and strollers are not allowed in some exhibition venues.

Dis. access

▪ Same-day free admission to the Legion of Honor museum *(see p117)*.

TOP 10 ★ San Francisco Museum of Modern Art

Founded in 1935, the SFMOMA is devoted to collecting and exhibiting modern and contemporary art. It is currently closed while it undergoes a massive building expansion, offering more public areas and educational facilities, and flexible gallery space for its growing collection. Until its reopening in 2016, exhibitions of the collection will be on view at, and given on loan to, partner museums around the city.

1 Roof Garden
Featuring a combination of well-known and rarely seen works from the museum's collection, this garden is not to be missed.

2 Photography
One of the museum's strengths; exhibits may include masterpieces by Man Ray, Ansel Adams, and Edward Weston, plus more avant-garde works.

3 Exterior
The building was designed by Mario Botta. The 125-ft (38-m) truncated turret **(below)** is decorated with Art Deco-style chevrons.

4 Latin American Artists
Latin American art is represented most forcefully in the museum by the work of muralist Diego Rivera and his wife Frida Kahlo. Other Latin American painters represented include Wilfredo Lam and Joaquín Torres-García.

5 Electronic and Digital Art
Established in 1987, the collection includes multi-media works, moving-image pieces, and video installations by such artists as Brian Eno, Dara Birnbaum, Bill Viola, and Nam June Paik.

6 The Catwalk
Suspended high up inside the cylindrical turret, visitors can walk the see-through 35-ft (10-m) steel bridge that cuts across the skylight **(above)**, providing dramatic views of both the Sculpture Terrace and the Atrium.

7 Temporary Exhibitions
The museum's temporary exhibition spaces may include educational programs, retrospective exhibitions of the work of contemporary artists such as Yoko Ono and Eva Hesse, or the photography of the Victorian author Lewis Carroll.

SFMOMA Floorplan

Key
First floor
Second floor
Third floor
Fourth floor
Fifth floor

Temporary Exhibitions **7**

The Catwalk **6**

Electronic & Digital Art **5**

Temporary Exhibitions **7**

Photography **2**

Bay Area Artists **10**

Latin American Artists **4**

Photography **2**

20th-Century European Artists **8**

20th-Century American Artists **9**

Roof Garden **1**

Exterior **3**

8 20th-Century European Artists

These works are located on the second floor. Here you will find important works by Matisse, Miró, Degas, Picasso, Braque, Klee, Mondrian, Duchamp, Dalí, and Magritte, among others.

9 20th-Century American Artists

US artists included here are O'Keeffe, de Kooning, Pollock, Warhol, and Kline. One of the perennial hits **(right)** is Jeff Koons' iconic ceramic sculpture *Michael Jackson and Bubbles* (1988).

10 Bay Area Artists

San Francisco Bay Area artists on display include Clyfford Still, Richard Diebenkorn, and Wayne Thiebaud, all with international reputations. Bay Area figurative painters in the collection include Elmer Bischoff and David Park. Most noteworthy, perhaps, is *California Artist* (1982), a sculptural self-portrait by Robert Arneson in glazed stoneware.

NEED TO KNOW

MAP Q5 ■ 151 3rd St ■ (415) 357-4000 ■ www.sfmoma.org

Currently closed for major renovations until 2016.

Adm $18 adult, $12 senior, $11 student with ID, free child 0–12 years; audio tour price varies; free first Tue of month, half-price on Thu evenings

Dis. access

Museum store: 51 Yerba Buena Lane (between Market and Mission Sts). (415) 357-4035. 11am–7pm Mon–Sat, noon–5pm Sun

■ The museum store will remain open during the renovation, but based in a temporary location.

■ Across 3rd Street from SFMOMA, Yerba Buena Gardens *(see pp32–3)* offers more galleries, museums, and attractions.

Museum Guide

The museum renovation project will see SFMOMA increase its size to 225,000 sq ft (20,903 sq m). This will include a larger gallery for their increasing permanent collection of art. The third-floor outdoor sculpture terrace will have the world's biggest public living wall, in the form of a large-scale vertical garden. Live art, film screenings, and events will take place on the fourth floor, and a conservation studio will stretch over the seventh and eighth floors.

Yerba Buena Gardens

Skyscrapers around Yerba Buena Gardens

1 Yerba Buena Center for the Arts Gallery

MAP Q5 ▪ 701 Mission St ▪ (415) 978-2787 ▪ Open noon–8pm Thu–Sat, noon–6pm Sun ▪ Dis. access ▪ Adm ▪ www.ybca.org

Changing exhibitions here explore issues of race, class, gender, history, technology, and art.

2 Yerba Buena Center for the Arts Theater

MAP Q5 ▪ Box Office: (415) 978-2787

Multiculturalism is often the keynote in this 750-seat indoor theater, so that the range of performances could include world-music festivals or Victorian operettas.

3 Moscone Center

MAP Q5 ▪ Howard St

This building began the renovation of the SoMa district. Most of it is under-ground; above ground the impression is of glass, girders, and gardens.

4 Metreon

MAP Q4 ▪ 101 4th St

The main attraction at this shopping center is a state-of-the-art cineplex (including IMAX screens). On the fourth floor is a pleasant terrace with superb views of the cityscape.

5 Rooftop Children's Center and Carousel

MAP Q5 ▪ 750 Folsom St

The carousel in this complex dates from 1906. There's also an ice-skating rink, a bowling alley, a learn-ing garden, and an amphitheater.

6 Children's Creativity Museum

MAP Q5 ▪ 221 4th St ▪ (415) 820-3320 ▪ Open 10–4pm Wed–Sun ▪ Dis. access ▪ Adm ▪ www.creativity.org

This interactive technology and art museum aims to inspire children's creative impulses. There are anim-ation, design, and music studios.

7 California Historical Society Museum

MAP P5 ▪ 678 Mission St ▪ (415) 357-1848 ▪ Open noon–5pm Tue–Sun ▪ Donations

This research organization holds vast collections of photos, books, maps, manuscripts, prints, and arts, some dating as far back as the 1600s.

8 Martin Luther King, Jr. Memorial

Featuring words of peace in several languages, this multifaceted monument incorporates sculpture, a waterfall, and quotations from the speeches and writings of the Civil Rights leader.

(9) Contemporary Jewish Museum (CJM)

MAP P5 ▪ 736 Mission St between 3rd and 4th ▪ (415) 655-7800 ▪ Open 1–8pm Thu, 11am–5pm Fri–Tue ▪ Closed Wed, Jewish hols & some public hols ▪ Dis. access ▪ Adm ▪ www.thecjm.org

This dynamic museum was designed by architect Daniel Libeskind and incorporates the landmark Jesse Street Power Substation. Its exhibitions help to foster relations with the wider community.

Contemporary Jewish Museum

(10) Esplanade

The Esplanade comprises garden-lined walkways, an inviting lawn, rolling hills, trees, and interesting sculptures. There is a free weekly concert here during the summer festival *(www.ybae.org)*.

THE RISE OF SOUTH OF MARKET

Formerly a doggedly industrial area full of warehouses and factories, this flat stretch attracted few residents. For nearly 100 years, it was considered unattractive, if not downright dangerous. All that began to change in the 1970s, when slums were cleared away and the Moscone Center was built. Upscale interior designer showrooms soon followed; ensuing decades brought premier nightclubs, and the digital boom added more than virtual life to the place. Public structures have sprung up, and the whole district is now seen as a desirable neighborhood – at least for creative types.

TOP 10
NOTABLE CONSTRUCTIONS SOUTH OF MARKET

1 AT&T Park
2 SFMOMA
3 Moscone Center
4 Yerba Buena Center
5 Rincon Center
6 Metreon
7 South Park
8 The Galleria
9 Ed Hardy San Francisco
10 The Four Seasons and the Marriott hotels

The Moscone Center, which was completed in 1981, began the rejuvenation of the South of Market district.

TOP 10 ⭐ Mission Dolores

The Misión San Francisco de Asís acquired its popular name, Mission Dolores, from a nearby stream, Arroyo de Nuestra Señora de los Dolores. It is the oldest building in the city and the oldest intact mission chapel in the chain of 21 established under Franciscan friar Junípero Serra's direction. The site was founded in 1776. The chapel was built between 1782 and 1791, with the labor of Ohlone people. Its adobe walls are 4 ft (1.2 m) thick and its red-tile roofs are typical of the "Mission Style" seen all over California in both old and new buildings.

1 Dolores Park
One of the few large green spaces in the Mission District, this park **(below)** is high on a hill and affords excellent views of the city. It was originally the site of San Francisco's main Jewish cemetery, but was transformed in 1905.

2 Beamed Ceiling Decoration
The imaginative painted ceiling design derives from Ohlone basketry.

3 Altarpieces
The reredos and side altars came from Mexico in the late 1700s and early 1800s.

4 Stations of the Cross
These images depicting each of the 14 Stations of the Cross, are distributed throughout the basilica, and were created by the artisan Samuel Berger.

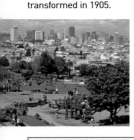

5 Chapel
The central building **(above)** still retains the original redwood beams, lashed together with rawhide. The amber-colored glass in the windows gives the interior a warmth that is reflected off the gold-leafed fixtures.

6 Cemetery and Serra Statue
This historic cemetery is the resting place of 5,000 Ohlone people who built the Mission, as well as many of San Francisco's early leaders. Central to the space is a life-size sculpture of Father Junípero Serra **(left)**.

NEED TO KNOW

MAP F5 ▪ 3321 16th St at Dolores St ▪ (415) 621-8203 ▪ missiondolores.org

Open 9am–4pm daily

Suggested donation $5 adult, $3 child

▪ For a fresh, authentic taste of Mexico, head for Pancho Villa Taqueria *(see p115)*.

▪ Check out the old photos in the covered walkway on the right side of the chapel, which depict, among other things, early Native American festivals and the total destruction in 1906 of the church next door, which was replaced by the basilica.

Mission Facade 7

The modest white facade of the chapel **(right)** is typical of the Mission Style. Its four columns support niches for three bronze bells added in the late 18th century, which are inscribed with the dates they were made.

JUNÍPERO SERRA AND CALIFORNIA'S MISSIONS

In 1769, Gaspar de Portola led an expedition to establish missions in California, with Father Junípero Serra and 60 other men. They founded Mission San Diego, and then worked their way up to Monterey. Continuing along up the coast, within seven years Father Serra had established a mission in San Francisco with Father Francisco Palou. In all, Father Serra founded nine missions in Upper California between 1769 and 1784. His successors went on to found 12 missions between 1786 and 1823.

Diorama and Museum 10

Just outside the chapel is a diorama showing what life was like at the mission two centuries ago. A museum at the back of the chapel contains artifacts and reproductions of Native American life.

Dolores Street 8

Undulating like a roller coaster, this is one of the loveliest streets in all of San Francisco. Palm trees grace its center, all the way along the length of it.

Choir Windows of St. Francis 9

Jewel-like stained-glass windows **(below)** depict the life of St. Francis, patron saint of San Francisco. The lower side windows depict the 21 California Missions.

Mission Dolores Floorplan

The Wine Country

The world-famous Wine Country comprises two picturesque valleys, Napa and Sonoma, the hills and dales surrounding them, and over 300 wineries. Napa is more developed for visitors, while Sonoma is more low-key but equally inviting. Both are convenient for a day trip, but it's worth spending a night or two – not only for the wine but also to enjoy the hot springs *(see pp38–9)*.

1 Napa Valley Train

Leaving from Napa and arriving in St. Helena, or vice versa, you can avoid the traffic and partake of a gourmet meal complemented by local wines. The trip takes 3 hours in total and the train **(below)** features a 1915 Pullman dining car.

2 Sterling Vineyard

There's a good self-guided tour at this mountain-top vineyard.

3 Beringer Vineyards

The oldest and the most beautiful Napa Valley winery **(below)**, established in 1876. Tours include a visit to the 1,000-ft (300-m) wine tunnels, which Chinese laborers carved out of volcanic stone.

4 Clos Pegase

Housed in an award-winning Post-Modern structure, this beguiling winery offers free tours and features an extensive collection of modern art. The wine is memorable, too – specialties include Cabernet, Merlot, and Petite Sirah port.

5 Yountville

Hot-air balloons float in the sky over the village of Yountville, where sweet cottages share the tree-lined streets with restaurants, galleries, upscale hotels, and V Marketplace, a gigantic brick edifice that houses shops, cafés, a spa, and wine-tasting salons.

Map of the Wine Country

6 The Culinary Institute of America

An impressive castle-like landmark, built in about 1890, houses the West Coast annex of the Culinary Institute of America. Foodies can stock up at the gourmet store, peruse the museum, or enjoy cookery and wine classes. The restaurant, with a terrace overlooking the vineyard, serves regional cuisine paired with appropriate wines.

7 Sonoma
This appealing town, nestled in the Valley of the Moon **(below)**, is filled with high-end restaurants, small hotels, and shops. The town also features a State Historic Park with a mission building and structures from the early to mid-1800s.

CALIFORNIA WINE
Since 1857, wine-making has been the mainstay of this area. A phylloxera blight in the early 1900s nearly put an end to it all, but Europe was hit harder, and it was the resistant California vines that brought back the wine business to parts of Italy, France, and Spain. In 1976 California wines were put on the international map, when they trounced France in a blind taste-test in Paris. These days, many European producers also have wineries in California.

10 Hess Collection
The tours here are a pleasure, including not only wine-making facilities but also the owner's gallery of contemporary European and American artists. The Cabernet Sauvignon, Merlot, and Chardonnay **(right)** are all very good.

8 Domaine Chandon
Lovely gardens, a fine restaurant, and sweeping views complement the sparkling, champagne-style wines of this Moët Hennessy showcase, which produces 500,000 cases every year.

9 Castello di Amorosa
This re-creation of a Medieval castle has a moat and a drawbridge as well as a torture chamber. Take a guided tour and taste V. Sattui wines, which are produced here.

NEED TO KNOW

Beringer Vineyards: 2000 Main St, St. Helena ■ (707) 963-4812 ■ www.beringer.com

Castello di Amorosa: 4045 St. Helena Hwy, Calistoga ■ (707) 967-6272 ■ www.castellodiamorosa.com

Clos Pegase: 1060 Dunaweal Lane ■ (707) 942-4981 ■ www.clospegase.com

The Culinary Institute of America: 2555 Main St, St. Helena ■ (707) 967-2320 ■ www.ciachef.edu

Domaine Chandon: 1 California Drive, Yountville ■ (707) 944-2280 ■ www.chandon.com

Hess Collection: 4411 Redwood Rd, Napa ■ (707) 255-1144 ■ www.hesscollection.com

Napa Valley Wine Train: 1275 McKinstry St, Napa ■ (707) 253-2111 ■ www.winetrain.com

Sterling Vineyard: 1111 Dunaweal Lane ■ (800) 726-6136 ■ www.sterlingvineyards.com

■ For very special snacks try the Model Bakery at 1357 Main St in St. Helena.

Wine Country Spas

1 Fairmont Sonoma Mission Inn & Spa

100 Boyes Blvd, Boyes Hot Springs ▪ **(707) 938-9000** ▪ **www.fairmont.com/sonoma**

This famous inn provides an oasis of ultimate indulgence in luxury and refinement. Blessed by natural mineral hot springs, the legendary spa, with inspired architecture and lovely landscaping, exudes understated opulence and serenity.

Fairmont Sonoma Mission Inn & Spa

2 Indian Springs Calistoga

1712 Lincoln Ave, Calistoga ▪ **(707) 942-4913** ▪ **www.indianspringscalistoga.com**

Dating from 1862, this hot springs resort with mineral waters from natural geysers was recently modernized but has an old-fashioned air about it, with an Olympic-sized heated pool, a clay tennis court, and professional spa and mud bath treatments. On-site are lodge rooms and pretty cottages with fireplaces, kitchens, and air-conditioning. There's also a casual eatery and bar.

3 Health Spa Napa Valley

1030 Main St, St. Helena ▪ **(707) 967-8800** ▪ **www.napavalleyspa.com**

In a serene, open-air setting, guests can yield aches and anxiety to a plethora of pampering and invigorating rituals. For some, that may mean a stimulating fitness workout, or a soothing mud wrap and massage overlooking the tranquil Spa Garden.

4 The Kenwood Inn and Spa

10400 Sonoma Hwy, Kenwood ▪ **(707) 833-1293** ▪ **www.kenwoodinn.com**

Nationally acclaimed as one of the Wine Country's most elegant and intimate country inns, the Kenwood consists of lovely guest suites and a full-service spa facility. The inn has the ambience of an Italian country villa in the Sonoma Valley, situated on a secluded hillside facing over 1,000 acres (404 ha) of vineyards. The spa offers a variety of massage styles, including aromatherapy and Ayurvedic.

5 Calistoga Spa Hot Springs

1006 Washington St, Calistoga ▪ **(707) 942-6269** ▪ **www.calistogaspa.com**

Just off the main street, soak in the four outdoor geothermal mineral pools (with a wading pool for kids). Try a mud bath, work out in the gym, or take a yoga or Pilates class. Recent renovations have given rooms a comfortable contemporary feel.

6 Mount View Hotel & Spa

1457 Lincoln Ave, Calistoga ▪ **(707) 942-5789** ▪ **www.mountviewhotel.com**

A stay in this historic 1917 resort offers various relaxation and rejuvenation possibilities – mud, milk, or herbal baths, aromatherapy steam showers, body wraps, massages, or facials – geared to individuals or couples.

⑦ Meritage Resort and Spa
875 Bordeaux Way, Napa ▪ (707) 251-1900 ▪ www.meritageresort.com

Silence and serenity abide in this luxury resort. The stone-walled, Old World-style "Estate Cave" contains 12 treatment rooms, with whirlpools and saunas. The four-star hotel rooms are spacious; ask about the special packages on offer. On site, you will find restaurants, a large fitness studio, and a sports bar.

Meritage Resort and Spa

⑧ Silverado Resort and Spa
1600 Atlas Peak Rd, Napa ▪ (707) 257-0200 ▪ www.silveradoresort.com

On 1,200 acres (485 ha), studded by oak trees and anchored by a historic mansion housing restaurants and lounges, the largest resort in the Wine Country has two championship golf courses, dozens of swimming pools, and a tennis complex. The upscale spa offers 12 rooms for top-notch body treatments, plus private garden pavilions, a nail and hair salon, a café, yoga classes, and workout facilities.

⑨ Villagio Inn and Spa
6481 Washington St, Yountville ▪ (707) 944-8877 ▪ www.villagio.com

Fireplaces, water features, and lush gardens create rustic luxury, to be enjoyed in the 16 treatment rooms with Swiss showers, saunas, and secluded outdoor baths. Spa suites for couples are romantic enclosures with soaking tubs, fireplaces, steam showers, and private terraces. At the associated four-star Villagio Inn, spacious rooms are surrounded by gardens adorned with replicas of Greek and Roman statuary.

⑩ Boon Hotel and Spa
14711 Armstrong Woods Rd, Guerneville ▪ (707) 869-2721 ▪ www.boonhotels.com

Located in the beautiful Russian River area, this peaceful spot in the Sonoma County redwoods offers an invigorating retreat from modern life. Body treatments include deep-tissue massages, hot-stone massages, and soothing facials with seaweed anti-wrinkle masks. Included in your stay are use of the pool and Jacuzzi, and evening wine-tastings on selected weekends. The restaurant serves Russian River wines, and sources ingredients from local suppliers or from its garden.

Championship golf course at Silverado Resort and Spa

The Top 10 of Everything

Interior of Grace Cathedral

🔟 Moments in History

Depiction of Native American hunters in San Francisco Bay

1 Native Americans
There were settlements in the Bay as early as the 11th century BC, made up of hunters and gatherers who enjoyed a rich diet of seeds, shellfish, and game. Historians group these peoples into the Coast Miwok, the Wintun, and the Ohlone.

2 Sir Francis Drake
In 1579, the English privateer landed near Point Reyes and claimed Alta California for Queen Elizabeth I. Along with other early explorers of the area, he failed to notice the marvelous bay just inside the straits. England didn't follow up its claim to Northern California, leaving it to the Spanish to conquer.

Drawing of gold seekers landing in San Francisco, 1849

3 Spanish Control
About 200 years after Drake's wanderings, Spain got serious about establishing a presence in Alta California. In 1776, an expedition led by Juan Bautista de Anza arrived at San Francisco Bay and established the Presidio (fort). A mission was also founded by Father Junípero Serra *(see pp34–5)*.

4 American Takeover
Impending war with Mexico in the 1840s inspired US leaders to arouse the interest of Bay Area settlers in joining the Union. In 1846, a party of Yankees in Sonoma declared California's independence from Mexico, christening it the Bear Flag Republic. Shortly after, Commodore John Sloat claimed California as US territory.

5 Gold Rush Days
In 1848 landowner John Sutter noticed a curious glitter in the sediment of the American River in the Sierra Nevada foothills and realized it was gold. Despite attempts to keep the discovery quiet, word leaked out, and businessman Sam Brannan displayed a bottle of gold dust and nuggets for the whole

city to see. The subsequent stampede of '49ers turned the city into a boomtown overnight.

6 Wells Fargo

The stagecoaches of Wells Fargo & Co began carrying freight and passengers in 1852, taking full advantage of the momentum created by the Gold Rush. It was also instrumental in the development of the Pony Express (see p53).

7 Panama-Pacific Exposition

Held in 1915 to celebrate the opening of the Panama Canal, the real *raison d'être* for the festivities was that San Franciscans had resurrected their city after the 1906 disaster.

8 Bay and Golden Gate Bridges

The inauguration of the Bay Bridge in 1936 heralded the end of the age of ferryboats by linking the city to the East Bay. The inauguration of the Golden Gate Bridge (see pp12–13) took place a year later.

9 "Summer of Love"

San Francisco counterculture burst forth in the summer of 1967. Hippies were everywhere, and the poetic music that embodied a new way of thinking filled the air. It was a sociopolitical shift that went on to affect the whole world.

10 Modern Politics

California has always been a few steps ahead of the rest of the United States. In 1992 it became the first state to send two female Senators, Dianne Feinstein and Barbara Boxer, to the US Congress, while Nancy Pelosi was the first ever female Speaker of the House of Representatives from 2007 to 2011.

Dianne Feinstein

TOP 10 SCANDALS AND DISASTERS

The ruins of the 1906 earthquake

1 Native Americans' Near-Extinction
In the late 1800s Native Americans were hunted down by settlers, with a bounty paid for each scalp.

2 Gold Rush Lawlessness
Gold Rush frontier life was so criminal that vigilante justice was proclaimed in the 1850s, leading to secret trials.

3 1906
An earthquake and consequent fire devastated much of the city, and 250,000 people were left homeless.

4 "Bloody Thursday"
On July 5, 1934, the police fired shots at longshoremen who were on strike, leaving two of them dead.

5 Howl
On October 13, 1955, Allen Ginsberg read his revolutionary poem, which was later banned as obscene, at the Six Gallery in San Francisco.

6 Freedom and Anti-War Riots
Pro-Civil Rights and anti-Vietnam War riots occurred from 1964 to 1970.

7 Death of a Rock Icon
Part of hippie legend, Janis Joplin died of a heroin overdose in 1970.

8 White's Revenge
In 1978 ex-Supervisor Dan White shot dead Mayor George Moscone and gay Supervisor Harvey Milk (see p47). He was controversially convicted of manslaughter rather than murder.

9 AIDS
The epidemic reached overwhelming proportions in the city in the 1980s.

10 Loma Prieta Earthquake
In October 1989, the quake destroyed the Victorian center of Santa Cruz (see p65) and part of the Bay Bridge.

Writers and Notable Residents

"Beat" author Jack Kerouac

1 Jack Kerouac

Arriving from New York in 1947, it was Kerouac (1922–69) who coined the term "Beat." He and his companions – Neal Cassady, Allen Ginsberg, Lawrence Ferlinghetti, and others – initiated the new politics of dissent and free love that led, within a decade, to the hippie movement (see p43). His novel *On the Road* (1957) galvanized a generation.

2 Isabel Allende

One of the world's most widely read Spanish-language authors, this Chilean-American Bay Area resident is famous for her magic realism in *The House of the Spirits*, *City of the Beasts*, *Eva Luna*, and *Of Love and Shadows*. She received the Presidential Medal of Freedom in 2014.

3 Robin Williams

A resident of the Bay Area from when he was a teenager, TV and movie star Williams (1951–2014) began his career as a stand-up comedian in San Francisco clubs and was credited with kick-starting the comedy "renaissance" of the 1970s. Beloved by and friendly to locals, he was known for his generosity to Bay Area charities.

4 William Randolph Hearst

A flamboyant publisher of the *San Francisco Examiner* who built the nation's largest newspaper chain in the late 1800s, Hearst (1863–1951) influenced the American press with his "yellow journalism" tactics, built Hearst Castle, served twice in the House of Representatives, and inspired the movie *Citizen Kane*.

5 Francis Ford Coppola

The director of *The Godfather* makes San Francisco the home of his American Zoetrope productions, and has also branched out into other enterprises. His Inglenook winery in the Napa Valley is one of the best.

6 Jack London

Adventurer and author of frontier tales such as *White Fang*, *The Sea Wolf*, and *The Call of the Wild*, Jack London (1876–1916) grew up in Oakland. A museum of his memorabilia is now housed there, in a reconstruction of the log cabin he lived in while prospecting for gold in the Yukon territory. His fiction is based on his experiences in the untamed West and the social inequality he saw in boomtown San Francisco.

Jack London statue

7 Dashiell Hammett

The author of *The Maltese Falcon* and creator of the classic hard-boiled detective Sam Spade lived in San Francisco from 1921 to 1929. He used the fog-swirled slopes of the hills as the backdrop for his crime stories. Hammett (1894–1961) was himself employed briefly at the famous Pinkerton Detective Agency.

8 Armistead Maupin

Maupin's *Tales of the City* were serialized in the *San Francisco Chronicle* before being published in book form. They are lighthearted paeans to the idiosyncrasies of gay San Francisco in the 1970s, before AIDS changed everything.

9 Carlos Santana

A Mexican-American who grew up in San Francisco and was influenced by Bay Area 1960s jazz and folk musicians, Santana founded a band that pioneered Afro-Latin-blues-rock fusion at the Fillmore West, in other area clubs, and at Woodstock. He went on to top the *Billboard* charts for decades, selling more than 100 million records.

Carlos Santana in concert

10 Joe DiMaggio

DiMaggio (1914–99) was born and began his baseball career in San Francisco. His 56-game hitting streak with the New York Yankees made him a legend. He married Marilyn Monroe in San Francisco.

Baseball player Joe DiMaggio

TOP 10 SIXTIES FIGURES

Janis Joplin

1 Janis Joplin
This troubled singer from Texas was the queen of the San Francisco sound, until her death by heroin overdose.

2 Ken Kesey
A powerful, revolutionary writer, his Magic Bus and Trips Festival set the tone for the entire hippie movement.

3 Jerry Garcia
Patriarch of the San Francisco sound, his Grateful Dead band continued to tour until his death in 1995.

4 Mario Savio
The UC Berkeley student launched the Free Speech Movement on the campus in the late 1960s.

5 Owsley Stanley
Stanley manufactured mass quantities of LSD and was the most famous source of pure LSD in the 1960s.

6 Grace Slick
The other queen of the San Francisco sound, fronting Jefferson Airplane.

7 Huey Newton
Oakland's founder of the Black Panthers, a group committed to change, by violence if necessary.

8 Patty Hearst
The newspaper heiress, kidnapped by the Symbionese Liberation Army in 1974, apparently converted and took part in an armed robbery.

9 Jim Jones
Leader of a cult that moved en masse to South America. He ended his days and those of some 900 followers in 1978, in a mass suicide caused by drinking cyanide-laced Kool-Aid.

10 Charles Manson
This commune leader and his followers murdered actress Sharon Tate in 1969.

ᴛᴏᴘ**10** Historic Sites

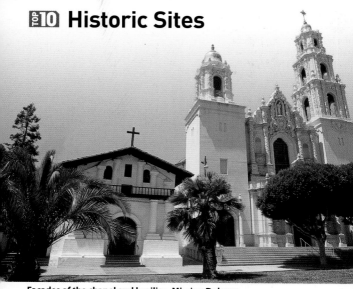

Facades of the chapel and basilica, Mission Dolores

1 Mission Dolores
This 18th-century Spanish mission, the area's earliest settlement, is worth a visit for its tranquillity and for an education on the city's history *(see pp34–5)*.

2 Jackson Square
This area contains some of the city's oldest, loveliest buildings. One of the few areas spared in the 1906 conflagration *(see p88)*.

3 Nob Hill
Home to historic hotels and remnants of the golden age of the railroad barons. The Fairmont Hotel (1907) is famous for the Tonga Room and Hurricane Bar, and the Mark Hopkins (1939) is crowned by the Top of the Mark lounge. Grace Cathedral's towers loom over all *(see p87)*.

4 The Presidio
More than 350 buildings, which spent 200 years in a military enclave, have been repurposed as museums, restaurants, and recreational facilities. Highlights are a National Cemetery, Civil War barracks, Victorian mansions, a World War II memorial, the Walt Disney Museum, the Society of California Pioneers Museum, and the heritage gallery in the Officers' Club *(see p98)*.

5 War Memorial Opera House
Inaugurated in 1932, this building is dedicated to World War I soldiers. In 1945 it hosted the plenary sessions that preceded the founding of the UN and, in 1951, it was the site of the signing of the peace treaty between the US and Japan *(see p68)*.

Huntington Park Fountain, Nob Hill

6 North Beach

This entire area resonates with the history of the early Italian residents, but even more with the iconoclastic legacy of the revolutionary Beats, who brought the neighborhood worldwide fame. Historic churches stand as clear landmarks, while equally historic saloons and cafés take a little snooping around to find (see p87).

7 Haight-Ashbury

The matrix of yet another bohemian movement that San Francisco has given birth to, this area nurtured idealistic hippies in the late 1960s. They brought international awareness to alternative ways of life, living in harmony with nature (see p104).

8 Fillmore Auditorium
MAP E3 ■ 1805 Geary Blvd

One of the legendary homes of psychedelic rock during the 1960s. Along with the Avalon Ballroom and the Winterland (both now gone), this is where the San Francisco sound found its first audience.

9 Ferry Building Marketplace

Once the tallest building in the city, with a 235-ft- (71.6-m-) high clock tower modeled after the Giralda tower in Seville, in 1898 this was the headquarters of countless streetcars and ferryboats. Fireboat crews saved the tower from the 1906 fire. Now, it's a huge food hall and marketplace (see p78).

10 Fort Point National Historic Site
MAP C1 ■ Marine Drive

At this much-photographed site under the Golden Gate Bridge, swords, guns, and cannons are on view at a fortification that was built during the Civil War to protect the city from an attack by sea, which never came. Rangers and costumed docents give free tours of the gunpowder storehouse, the barracks, and the museum.

TOP 10 HISTORIC FIGURES

John Muir

1 Junípero Serra
This 18th-century Spanish cleric traveled up and down California establishing missions, including Mission Dolores (see p34).

2 John C. Fremont
Instrumental in the US annexation of California in the mid-1800s, it was Fremont who dubbed the Bay strait the "Golden Gate."

3 John Muir
A keen promoter of the National Parks movement. The Muir Woods are named in his honor (see p64).

4 Leland Stanford
One of the "Big Four" who masterminded the Transcontinental Railroad, he also founded Stanford University (see p126).

5 Mark Hopkins
Another of the "Big Four" who struck it super-rich and lived on Nob Hill.

6 Charles Crocker
Another of the "Big Four." The Crocker Galleria recalls his legacy (see p78).

7 A. P. Giannini
Founder in 1904 of the Bank of Italy, later the Bank of America, Giannini financed the Golden Gate Bridge.

8 Harvey Milk
The first openly gay politician to become a member of the Board of Supervisors was assassinated in 1978.

9 Dianne Feinstein
One of the movers and shakers of San Francisco politics in recent decades, she became a US Senator in 1992.

10 Jerry Brown
The first three-term Governor of California and former Mayor of Oakland also ran for US President.

TOP 10 Churches

Cathedral of St. Mary of the Assumption

1 Cathedral of St. Mary of the Assumption

MAP F3 ■ 1111 Gough St ■ (415) 567-2020 ■ Services: 6:45am, 8am, 12:10pm Mon–Fri; 6:45am, 8am Sat; 7:30am, 9am, 11am, 1pm (Spanish), 5:30pm Sun ■ Dis. access

This 1971 building has been compared to a giant washing machine; inside is equally odd, with stained-glass strips and a sculpture of aluminum rods (see p50).

2 Grace Cathedral

The Notre Dame of San Francisco mixes Italian Renaissance with Gothic architecture and a lot of American originality (see p87).

3 St. Mark's Lutheran Church

MAP P1 ■ 1111 O'Farrell St ■ (415) 928-7770 ■ Services: 6:45pm Wed; 9am, 11am Sun ■ www.sfmarks-sf.org

This 1894 pink-brick church is a mixture of Gothic and Romanesque styles. After the 1906 earthquake (see p43), it served as a first-aid station and shelter.

4 Mission Dolores

Photos and a diorama offer a stirring impression of what life was like for the Native Americans who built this Spanish mission in the 18th century (see pp34–5).

5 St. Patrick's Cathedral

MAP Q4 ■ 756 Mission St ■ (415) 421-3730 ■ Services: 7:30am, 12:10pm, 5:15pm Mon–Sat; 7:30am, 9am, 10:30am, 12:15pm, 5:15pm Sun ■ www.stpatricksf.org

Constructed in 1872, this Gothic Revival cathedral has an impressive marble and stained-glass interior.

6 Glide Memorial United Methodist Church

MAP Q3 ■ 330 Ellis St ■ (415) 674-6000 ■ Services: 9am, 11am Sun ■ www.glide.org

This church has a credo of "the human condition first, not the Bible." Services can draw up to 1,500 celebrants, with a gospel choir. Same-sex couples can exchange vows of matrimony in this institution.

7 Saints Peter and Paul Church

North Beach's "Italian Cathedral" was once called the "Marzipan Church" for the stucco decoration on its soaring pinnacles. Inside, there is a sculpted reproduction of Leonardo da Vinci's Last Supper (see p92).

Stained glass, Saints Peter and Paul Church

8 Shrine of St. Francis of Assisi

MAP M4 ▪ 610 Vallejo St at Columbus ▪ (415) 986-4557 ▪ Services: 12:15pm Mon–Sat, 10am Sun ▪ www.shrinesf.org

Declared a National Historic Landmark, the Gothic Revival St. Francis of Assisi Church was established on June 17, 1849, as the first parish church in California. The interior is adorned with 11 larger-than-life murals, depicting the works of San Francisco's patron saint.

Art by Mark Dukes, St. John Coltrane Frican Orthodox Church

9 St. John Coltrane African Orthodox Church

MAP F3 ▪ St. Paul's Lutheran Church, 1286 Fillmore St ▪ (415) 673-7144 ▪ Services: noon Sun ▪ www.coltranechurch.org

"My music is the spiritual expression of what I am." So said jazz musician St. John Coltrane. Services consist of a performance of his *A Love Supreme* by the band Ohnedaruth and the Sisters of Compassion choir.

10 First Unitarian Universalist Church

MAP P1 ▪ 1187 Franklin St ▪ (415) 776-4580 ▪ Services: 11am Sun ▪ www.uusf.org

Since 1850, this church has been a progressive voice in San Francisco. Welcoming all faiths and creeds, this congregation is not bound by dogma, but by shared values.

TOP 10 OTHER PLACES OF WORSHIP

Exterior of Kong Chow Temple

1 Kong Chow Temple
Chinatown's oldest temple is dedicated to Kuan Di, a male deity *(see pp22–3)*.

2 Tin How Temple
The Queen of Heaven rules this sanctuary and makes sure devotees travel safely by water, among other things *(see p62)*.

3 Congregation Sherith Israel
MAP F3 ▪ 2266 California St ▪ Services: 6pm Fri, 10:30am Sat
Founded in 1849 by Jewish pioneers, the existing domed synagogue dates from 1904.

4 Vedanta Temple
MAP M5 ▪ 2323 Vallejo St
This was the first Hindu temple (1905) in the western US.

5 Zen Center
MAP F4 ▪ 300 Page St
Home to the city's Zen practitioners.

6 Crystal Way
MAP F5 ▪ 2335 Market St
Healing through crystals, light, sound, and positive thinking are explored.

7 Botanica Yoruba
All the Santería paraphernalia you'll need *(see p112)*.

8 Spirit Rock Meditation Center
5000 Sir Francis Drake Blvd, Woodacre, Marin
This center helps people find peace through meditation.

9 The Love of Ganesha
MAP E4 ▪ 1310 Haight St
Hindu clothing, arts, and crafts.

10 Open Secret
923 C St, San Rafael
The backroom of this New Age venue is like a temple to all the world's deities.

TOP 10 Architectural Highlights

Staircase of City Hall, Civic Center

in 1972. The color was a mistake – the granite that faces it was supposed to be pink, not brown, but by the time the delivery was made, it was too late to change it.

4 Xanadu Gallery
MAP P4 ▪ 140 Maiden Lane ▪ (415) 392-9999 ▪ Open 10am–6pm Tue–Sat ▪ www.folkartintl.com

Dating from 1948, this is the city's only building by Frank Lloyd Wright. The sweeping spiral ramp predates the one at Wright's Guggenheim Museum in New York.

5 Palace of Fine Arts
MAP E1 ▪ 3301 Lyon St ▪ (415) 563-6504 ▪ www.palaceoffinearts.org

This Neo-Classical building, today used for shows, was designed by Bernard Maybeck for the Pan-Pacific Exposition of 1915 and inspired by the engravings of Giovanni Piranesi.

1 Civic Center
This complex is centered on City Hall, a Baroque Revival master-piece (1915) with a golden dome, which attracts tourists and wedding parties for photos on its curving marble staircase decorated with filigree iron and gilt. The other core buildings are in Beaux Arts style, and befitting the city that started the Gold Rush, gilt is everywhere (see p89).

6 St. Mary's Cathedral
Some critics dismiss this parabolic form, but the soaring curves take attention upward, in the same way that tracery and vaulting do in Gothic cathedrals (see p48).

2 Transamerica Pyramid
MAP N5 ▪ 600 Montgomery St

Hated by many at first, the Pyramid is now loved as an icon of the city. To some it is a symbol of the mysticism that has always played a part in the San Francisco mentality. At 853 ft (260 m), it is the tallest building in the city, but its shape stops it casting a shadow on the neighborhood.

7 Coit Tower
Perched on Telegraph Hill, this Art Deco sentinel takes the form of a giant fluted column. Reminiscent of Renaissance towers, the column is 210 ft (64 m) tall and is perforated

3 Bank of America
MAP N5 ▪ 555 California St

This 52-story structure was the first skyscraper to be erected in the city,

Coit Tower, Telegraph Hill

around the top with arched openings and windows, which visitors can reach by elevator for stunning views of the city (see p92).

8 Grace Cathedral

The third largest Episcopal church in the US was executed in the medieval French Gothic style, echoing in particular Notre Dame in Paris, yet accomplished using steel-reinforced concrete (see p87).

Grace Cathedral

9 Haas-Lilienthal House

MAP M1 ▪ 2007 Franklin St ▪ (415) 441-3011 ▪ Open noon–3pm Sat & Wed, 11am–4pm Sun ▪ Adm

This Queen Anne-style mansion, built in 1886, is one of the few Victorian beauties in the city that accepts callers. It's a wonderful glimpse into the way of life among San Francisco's upper-middle classes from about 1890 to 1920. Outside, it features gables, a turret, and patterned embellishments; inside, you can see parlors, a dining room, bedrooms, and a ballroom.

10 Alamo Square

MAP E4

With a Downtown backdrop and a sweeping greensward below, these vividly hued late 1800s Victorian mansions (or "Painted Ladies") are on the 700 block of Steiner Street. The surrounding streets boast gems built between the 1870s and 1920s.

TOP 10 PUBLIC ART SITES

1 Balmy Alley
MAP G6 ▪ 24th & 25th Sts between Harrison & Treat
The most famous set of murals in town, by local Latino artists.

2 San Francisco Art Institute
MAP K3 ▪ 800 Chestnut St
Diego Rivera, the Mexican muralist, painted *The Making of a Fresco* here.

3 Coit Tower
Depression-era murals decorate the lobby (see p92).

4 Fort Mason
MAP J1 ▪ Franklin St
Oliver DiCicco's *Bow Seat* pays homage to small boats that have worked the Bay.

5 Women's Building
MAP F5 ▪ 18th St between Valencia & Guerrero
The work of seven women painters graces the facade.

6 Bikeway
MAP F4 ▪ Duboce St between Church & Market
This mural chronicles a bike ride from Downtown to Ocean Beach.

7 Beach Chalet
MAP A4 ▪ 1000 Great Hwy
Depression-era murals depicting famous citizens of San Francisco.

8 Rincon Center
MAP H2 ▪ Mission, Howard, Steuart & Spear Sts
These 1948 murals by Russian Anton Refregier trace Californian history.

9 Financial District
The black-stone *Transcendence* is in front of the Bank of America.

10 Golden Gate Park
The Music Concourse is home to many sculptures, including the bronze *Apple Cider Press* (see pp24–5).

Beach Chalet mural

🔟 Museums

1 de Young Museum

A bastion of American, Oceanian, and African art, the de Young is a landmark in Golden Gate Park, topped by a 144-ft (44-m) observation tower. Founded with pieces from the 1894 California Midwinter Fair, the Oceanic and African groupings have been expanded with private collections. There is a sculpture garden and a collection of American art from colonial times to the 20th century (see pp28–9).

2 California Academy of Sciences

The environmentally friendly architecture of the Academy building, which emphasizes ecological and sustainable features, blends with the natural surroundings of the park. The museum covers virtually every aspect of the natural world (see p25 and pp26–7).

3 Legion of Honor

MAP B3 ■ Lincoln Park, 34th Ave & Clement St ■ (415) 750-3600 ■ Open 9:30am–5:15pm Tue–Sun ■ Dis. access ■ Adm ■ www.famsf.org

This museum, located above Land's End, is one of the major venues for pre-modern art. It is also a beautiful building in a gorgeous natural

The Three Shades, **Legion of Honor**

setting, and well worth the time it takes to get here. It contains mostly European works, including masterpieces such as *The Three Shades* by Rodin and pieces by Rubens, Rembrandt, Georges de la Tour, Degas, and Monet.

4 Asian Art Museum

MAP R2 ■ 200 Larkin St ■ (415) 581-3500 ■ Open 10am–5pm Tue–Sun (10am–9pm Thu) ■ Adm ■ www.asianart.org

The Asian Art Museum is set in the entirely restructured and seismically retrofitted old Main Library in the Civic Center. The vast and important collection of Chinese, Korean, Japanese, Himalayan, and Southeast Asian works is displayed by country of origin. The layout also demonstrates the flow and

Korean costume, Asian Art Musuem

transformation of Buddhist art from India and outward into the entire Far East. Included is the fabulous Avery Brundage collection of Oriental jade.

⑤ San Francisco Museum of Modern Art

In 2016, a greatly expanded SFMOMA will open in the South of Market museum district. New additions include admission-free public areas, outdoor terraces, seven levels of 20th-century art, a café, and a large gift shop (see pp30–31).

⑥ San Francisco Museum of Craft and Design

MAP H5 ■ 2569 Third St ■ (415) 773-0303 ■ Open 11am–6pm Tue–Sat, noon–5pm Sun ■ Closed major public hols ■ Adm ■ www.sfmcd.org

This one-of-a-kind museum celebrates and promotes contemporary craft and design through innovative exhibitions and educational programs. Many lectures, special shows, and programs are organized to engage children, all designed to stimulate creativity. There is also a great museum store with many original, handmade pieces for sale.

⑦ Wells Fargo History Museum

MAP N5 ■ 420 Montgomery St ■ (415) 396-2619 ■ Open 9am–5pm Mon–Fri ■ www.wellsfargohistory.com/museums

Tales of the robbers who held up Wells Fargo stagecoaches are the stuff of legend. Exhibits here include Pony Express mail, gold nuggets, and Emperor Norton's currency (see p43).

⑧ Society of California Pioneers

MAP R5 ■ 300 4th St ■ (415) 957-1849 ■ Open 9am–noon Tue–Fri ■ Adm ■ www.californiapioneers.org

This museum displays a fascinating collection of historical exhibits from 19th- and 20th-century California. The upstairs gallery features an annually rotating exhibition of items from the private collection.

⑨ Contemporary Jewish Museum

MAP G3 ■ 736 Mission St ■ (415) 655-7800 ■ Open 11am–5pm Fri–Tue, 11am–8pm Thurs ■ Adm ■ www.thecjm.org

Across the street from Yerba Buena Gardens, this charming 1907 Willis Polk-designed power substation has been adapted by architect Daniel Libeskind, with soaring black glass blocks fronting the plaza. The small collection of contemporary and ancient Jewish artistic, historical, and cultural items is augmented by ever-changing exhibits encompassing political art, iconic Jewish figures, immigration, architecture, modern Israel, and more.

Contemporary Jewish Museum

⑩ Maritime Museum

MAP F1 ■ 900 Beach St, Aquatic Park ■ (415) 447-5000 ■ Open 10am–4pm daily ■ Dis. access ■ www.maritime.org

The 1939 bathhouse in which this museum is located was designed in the Streamline Moderne style, a late offshoot of the Art Deco period. Being modeled after the clean lines of an ocean liner, it looks for all the world like a cruise ship about to set sail into the Bay. Inside, it is awash with ship models, figureheads, maritime paintings, photos, and seagoing relics like scrimshaw, ships in bottles, and knot-tied folk art.

🔟 Art Galleries

① City Art Gallery

MAP F5 ▪ 828 Valencia St between 19th & 20th ▪ (415) 970-9900 ▪ Open noon–9pm Wed–Sun ▪ www.cityartgallery.org

Owned and operated by the artists themselves, this cooperative gallery prides itself on making artwork accessible and affordable to those interested in collecting art. Showcasing the work of around 200 local artists – some new, some known and established – the gallery exhibits an array of styles and media through changing exhibitions. Eighty percent of any sale goes directly to the artist.

② Gallery Wendi Norris

MAP P3 ▪ 161 Jessie St ▪ (415) 346-7812 ▪ Open 11am–6pm Tue–Sat ▪ www.freynorris.com

This dynamic and extremely stylish contemporary art venue in South of Market hosts exhibitions of celebrated American and international works, including those by prominent artists from China, Japan, South Korea, and Russia. Some Bay Area artists are also featured in the gallery. The staff is on hand to provide advice to amateur and serious collectors alike about the contemporary art market.

③ Pacific Heritage Museum

MAP N5 ▪ 608 Commercial St ▪ (415) 399-1124 ▪ Open 10am–4pm Tue–Sat

Occupying the old San Francisco Mint (1875–7), on top of which the East West Bank has been built. The bank sponsors the museum, which focuses on the art of the Pacific Rim, aiming to bring the work of Asian artists to a wider audience. Exhibitions feature many pieces on loan from private collections.

④ SoMarts Cultural Center

MAP G4 ▪ 934 Brannan St between 8th & 9th Sts ▪ (415) 863-1414 ▪ Open noon–7pm Tue–Fri, noon–5pm Sat ▪ www.somarts.org

Group and solo shows, music, and readings all take place here. Founded in 1975, SoMarts is a city-owned cultural center with two exhibition spaces, a 250-seat theater, and printmaking, photography, and design studios.

⑤ Fraenkel Gallery

MAP P4 ▪ 49 Geary St ▪ (415) 981-2661 ▪ Open 10:30am–5:30pm Tue–Fri, 11am–5pm Sat ▪ www.fraenkelgallery.com

Opened in 1979, the gallery held an exhibition early on of NASA's lunar photographs, and this set the tone for what followed. Soon came exhibitions by Eugene Atget, Edward Weston, Hiroshi Sugimoto, and Diane Arbus, and later, the Bechers, Adam Fuss, and Sol LeWitt. Projects have brought together work across all

Fraenkel Gallery

media, juxtaposing photography with painting, drawing, and sculpture. Other photographers whose work is regularly shown include Richard Avedon and Man Ray.

Display at Cartoon Art Museum

⑥ Cartoon Art Museum
MAP P5 ▪ 655 Mission St ▪ (415) 227-8666 ▪ Open 11am–5pm Tue–Sun ▪ Adm ▪ www.cartoonart.org

With an endowment from Peanuts creator, the late Charles M. Schulz, the museum is the only one in the US dedicated to cartoon art in all its forms. The museum's collection has approximately 6,000 pieces.

⑦ Museo Italo Americano
MAP F1 ▪ Fort Mason Center, Bldg C ▪ (415) 673-2200 ▪ Open noon–4pm daily (Mon by appointment only) ▪ www.museoitaloamericano.org

A museum, gallery, and community center for San Francisco's Italians. Regular changing temporary exhibitions might focus on the work of either an individual Italian artist, or on aspects of Italian culture. Classes are also offered at the center on Italian art history, culture, architecture, and cookery.

⑧ Galería de la Raza
MAP G5 ▪ 2857 24th St ▪ (415) 826-8009 ▪ Open noon–6pm Tue–Sat ▪ www.galeriadelaraza.org

Bimonthly exhibitions of Mexican-American art include painters, cartoonists, performance artists, muralists, or digital installations.

Programs are also held at the gallery, including films, panel discussions, and performances by stars of the Latino art and music scene.

⑨ Intersection for the Arts
MAP G3 ▪ 925 Mission St at 5th St ▪ (415) 626-2787 ▪ Open noon–6pm Tue–Sat ▪ www.theintersection.org

Radical and diverse art emerges from this hotbed of creativity. The alternative multi-genre art installation combines drama, video and film screenings, and panel discussions exploring the influence of race and relationships on people's work and lives.

⑩ San Francisco Arts Commission Gallery
MAP R1 ▪ 401 Van Ness Ave ▪ (415) 554-6080 ▪ Open noon–5pm Wed–Sat ▪ www.sfartscommission.org/gallery

Opened in 1970, this was one of the first galleries dedicated to showing the work of emerging Bay Area artists. In addition, the Gallery Slide Registry contains images by more than 500 professional artists from across the US.

🔟 **Parks and Gardens**

1 Marina Green
MAP E1

Within sight of the Golden Gate Bridge and across the street from photogenic 1930s mansions and the Palace of Fine Arts are several blocks of bayside greensward.

2 Golden Gate Park

One of the largest city parks in the US is also one of the most diverse, and all of it brought forth from what was once scrub and dunes. The park also features first-rate cultural attractions such as the de Young Museum *(see pp28–9)*.

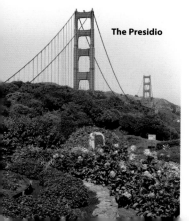

The Presidio

3 Fort Mason
MAP F1

The rolling lawn above Fort Mason Center *(see p99)*, known as the Great Meadow, is a relatively little-used park, but it's great for taking a siesta, tossing a frisbee, or just strolling through to take in the spectacular views from the cliffs.

4 The Presidio

This vast swath of greenery only entered the city's parklands in 1994. It is a beautiful space, and tourists and locals alike come to enjoy the wooded areas, walking trails, and wonderful views over the Bay *(see pp98–9)*. It is also home to chic restaurants and museums. Filmmaker George Lucas created a $350 million headquarters here for his production company Lucasfilm and up to 1,500 employees *(see p46)*.

5 Conservatory of Flowers
MAP D4

Shipped around Cape Horn from England and erected in Golden Gate Park in 1879, this magnificent five-story Victorian greenhouse contains a jungle of trees, palms, exotic plants, and flowers. There are thousands of orchids, an enchanting butterfly enclosure, and lily ponds.

The Victorian Conservatory of Flowers, Golden Gate Park

Plant lovers come from around the world to learn about endangered flora and horticultural innovations like aquascaping. *(See p24.)*

6 Alta Plaza
MAP E2

This double block of verdant hill in Pacific Heights is a popular place to take the sun when it ventures to break through the fog. Basketball and tennis courts and a children's playground are in the center, while to the south there are terraced lawns, onto which face some of the oldest homes in Pacific Heights.

Green oasis of Yerba Buena Gardens

7 Yerba Buena Gardens

In the South of Market museum district, surrounding the Yerba Buena Center for the Arts, are lawns, shade trees, gardens, and water features, which create a verdant setting for whimsical outdoor sculptures. Don't miss the 50-ft- (15-m-) wide Martin Luther King, Jr. waterfall *(see pp32–3)*.

8 Rincon Park
Map H2

Situated just south of the Ferry Building Marketplace on the Embarcadero pedestrian promenade, *Cupid's Span*, a 60-ft- (18-m-) tall sculpture of a red-feathered bow and arrow, marks the location of this bayside park. The lawns and benches afford awesome views of the San Francisco–Oakland Bay Bridge, the city skyline, and passing ships.

9 Lafayette Park
MAP F2

This is another of the double-blocked hilltop gardens in Pacific Heights – a leafy green haven of pine and eucalyptus trees. Steep stairways lead to the summit of the park, which has delightful views. The city did not manage to set aside these oases without a fight. Squatters' buildings occupied some of the land in the center of this park until as late as 1936, when they were finally pulled down, liberating the lush gardens for all to enjoy.

10 Sigmund Stern Recreation Grove

Famous for its free summer concerts, Sigmund Stern Recreation Grove is a leafy recreation complex containing playing fields, tennis and croquet courts, as well as a playground, and a dog park. Pine Lake is popular for jogging around, and there are plenty of good picnic spots under the eucalyptus, redwood, and pine trees.

ᴛᴏᴘ10 Beaches

Popular sands of Stinson Beach

1 Stinson Beach

Three miles (5 km) of sand, coupled with the fact that Marin County often has fine weather when the rest of the coast is covered in fog, make this one of the most popular beaches in the Bay Area. It can be crowded when it's sunny *(see p126)*.

2 Muir and Red Rock Beaches

Muir Beach: off Hwy 1 on Pacific Way
■ **Red Rock: 5.5 miles (9 km) north of Muir on Pacific Way**

These two beaches, just south of Stinson, are the most famous nude beaches north of San Francisco. Both are sandy curves within their own coves, protected from wind and prying eyes by rocky cliffs. The only caveat is that you'll need sturdy

The cliffs overlooking Muir Beach

walking shoes to get down the rough paths that lead to them from the parking lots.

3 China Beach

MAP B2

Officially called James D. Phelan Beach, this is the poshest beach in San Francisco, being an adjunct to the exclusive Sea Cliff neighborhood. Despite its pedigree, California law requires that all coastal areas remain public, although access roads to them can be private. China Beach is small and protected from the wind, there's plenty of parking, and it's a pleasant walk to the sand. You'll find showers and changing rooms.

4 Pacifica Beaches

Hwy 1

A 20-minute drive south of the city are several Pacific Ocean beaches popular with surfers, swimmers, and families. A favorite of beginner surfers, Linda Mar Beach has restrooms and showers, and connects by a breezy trail to Rockaway Beach. Sharp Park Beach has picnic sites, a fishing pier with a café, parking, and nature trails.

5 Bolinas Beach

This hidden-away Marin beach tends to be windy and is mostly used by dog-walkers and kayakers. It's sandy, with a backdrop of rocky cliffs. If you walk north, you'll find sheltered nooks, where some sun-worshippers bask in the nude, although there is a rarely enforced city ordinance against it *(see p127)*.

View of the Golden Gate Bridge from Baker Beach

6 Baker Beach
MAP C2

This 1-mile (1.5-km) stretch of sandy beach, with its perfect views of the Golden Gate Bridge, is the most popular in the city. It's great for sunbathing, dog-walking, picnicking, or jogging, but signs warn off swimmers because of riptides. The sunsets here are unforgettable.

7 Ocean Beach

Some 4 miles (6.5 km) long and quite broad, this is the city's largest beach by far, but probably the worst for entering the water safely. It starts at Cliff House and continues on beyond the city limits, turning into picturesque dunes at the southern end. Great for walking or jogging, and when the sun comes out, it's a fine place to sunbathe (see p117).

8 Marshall's Beach
MAP C1

Also known as Land's End Beach, diminutive Marshall's Beach is secluded almost beneath the Golden Gate Bridge, with stunning sea views and good sightings of seabirds. Be aware that this is the only nude beach in the city, and frequented by gay residents and freethinkers. Access is via the steep Batteries to Bluffs Trail, or from the north end of Baker Beach.

9 Aquatic Park
MAP F1

Shielded by a horseshoe-shaped fishing pier, this is a man-made lagoon near Fisherman's Wharf, with a calm cove, a sandy beach, a stepped seawall for lounging, restrooms, and a paved walkway making it accessible to wheelchairs and bikes. This is the number-one spot from which to watch the Fourth of July fireworks and Fleet Week aerial shows.

10 East Beach
MAP D1

On the paved Bay Trail between the yacht harbor in the Marina District and Crissy Field, with dazzling Golden Gate Bridge and Alcatraz views, this is one of the only beaches where swimming is safe from undertows and currents. On site are picnic tables and grills, restrooms, lawns for lounging, and free parking.

🔟 Outdoor Activities

A hiking trail on Mount Tamalpais

1 Hiking

The Bay Area is replete with magnificent hiking trails for every type of nature-lover. Land's End offers some wild terrain to scramble over *(see p119)*, and Mount Tamalpais is crisscrossed with trails *(see p126)*, but just scaling the city's hills is enough hiking for most people.

2 Swimming

MAP H2 ▪ Embarcadero YMCA: 169 Steuart St ▪ (415) 957-9622 ▪ www.ymcasf.org

Some hotels and the Embarcadero YMCA have pools, and close-to-shore swimming can be enjoyed at a few spots, namely China Beach, the protected cove at Aquatic Park, and the shallow waters off Crissy Field – kids wade in the tidal marsh here, too.

3 Sailing

www.ocscsailing.com

Charter a yacht or a masted schooner, take sailing lessons, or tour the Bay on a motor cruiser, catamaran, or sailboat. Fun to watch are the frequent regattas and boating events, from Opening Day on the Bay to Fleet Week and the Fourth of July.

4 In-line Skating

Golden Gate Park and in-line skaters make a perfect match, especially on Sundays, when the main street in the park is closed to cars. Or try the smoothly paved path that runs along Marina Green.

5 Running

Bay to Breakers: 3rd Sun in May ▪ (415) 864-3432 ▪ www.bayto breakers.com; San Francisco Marathon: Jun or Jul ▪ (888) 958-6668 ▪ www.thesfmarathon.com

Since the restoration of Crissy Field, the Golden Gate Promenade *(see p98)* has been an inspiring run – and, of course, Golden Gate Park offers endless opportunities for jogging. If organized running is your thing, try the Bay to Breakers or the San Francisco Marathon.

6 Tennis

San Francisco Recreation and Park Department: (415) 831-2700 ▪ Golden Gate Park: (415) 753-7001

Contact the Recreation and Park Department for your nearest free public tennis court. Golden Gate Park courts charge a small fee, but you can book in advance. Most public outdoor courts are open from sunrise to sunset. Indoor courts are the purview of private tennis clubs, with membership required.

Sailing in the Bay

7 Golf

Golden Gate Park: (415) 751-8987 ■ **Lincoln Park:** (415) 221-9911 ■ **Presidio Golf Course:** (415) 561-4661 ■ **TPC Harding Park:** (415) 664-4690

TPC Harding Park has been modernized for professional tournaments, and Presidio Golf Course is among the best in the country. Locals love Lincoln Park, an affordable track above Land's End; the par 3 Golden Gate Park Golf Course; and the nine-hole Gleneagles Golf Course.

Biking near the Golden Gate Bridge

8 Biking

City Cycle: 3001 Steiner St ■ (415) 346-2242 ■ www.citycycle.com

Although the hills overwhelm all but those with legs of steel, bicycling is very big in San Francisco. Don't miss biking across the Golden Gate Bridge. Rent bikes from City Cycle.

9 Boating

Sailing, rowing, and kayaking are all great here, although far from easy on the Bay's unpredictable waters and in its sometimes ferocious winds. Play it safe by taking a boat out on Stow Lake in Golden Gate Park *(see p24)*.

10 Windsurfing

The Bay is one of the most popular windsurfing and kiteboarding sites in the world, creating excitement for spectators along the shoreline, too. Boardsports shops offer lessons and rentals.

TOP 10 SPECTATOR SPORTS

Levi's Stadium, home of the 49ers

1 San Francisco 49ers
4900 Marie P. DeBartolo Way, Santa Clara ■ (415) 656-4900
NFL team, plays September to January.

2 San Francisco Giants
AT&T Park, 24 Willie Mays Plaza ■ (415) 972-2000
Baseball team, plays April to October.

3 Golden State Warriors
Oakland Arena, 7000 Coliseum Way, Oakland ■ (510) 986-2222
An NBA basketball team.

4 Oakland Athletics
(510) 638-0500
Historic winners of the American Football League in the 1970s.

5 Oakland Raiders
(800) 724-3377
American Football League team.

6 Golden Gate Fields
1100 Eastshore Highway, Berkeley ■ (510) 559-7300
The East Bay venue for horse-racing.

7 Mazda Raceway Laguna Seca
1021 Monterey–Salinas Hwy, Salinas ■ (831) 242-8201
Grand Prix and motorcycle racing at this 2.2-mile (3.6-km) track.

8 Sonoma Raceway
Hwys 37 & 121, Sonoma ■ (707) 938-8448
Superbike and auto-racing in the Sonoma Valley.

9 San Jose Sharks
HP Pavilion, 525 West Santa Clara St, San Jose ■ (800) 888-2736
Fast-paced NHL ice hockey.

10 Sacramento Kings
Power Balance Pavilion, 1 Sports Parkway, Sacramento ■ (916) 928-0000
Men's NBA basketball team.

🔟 Off the Beaten Path

The Lyon Street steps, leading into the Presidio

1 Lyon Street Steps
MAP E2 ▪ Lyon St at Broadway

Take your time climbing the Lyon Street steps adjacent to the Presidio (there are over 200) for sweeping, bird's-eye views of the Bay, the Presidio, the Palace of Fine Arts, and the manicured gardens and balconied perfection of the Pacific Heights mansions. At the top there is a gate into the Presidio.

2 Tin How Temple
MAP N4 ▪ 125 Waverly Place ▪ (415) 986-2520 ▪ Open 10am–4pm daily

On a Chinatown backstreet in a colorful 19th-century building, a narrow stairway leads past a mah-jongg parlor to the Tin How Temple, where incense wafts through a lantern-lit chamber dedicated to the Queen of Heaven. Be respectful, and burn a joss stick for your fortune.

3 Angel Island State Park
Belvedere Tiburon ▪ www.angelislandsf.com ▪ Café open 10am–3pm Mon–Fri, 10am–4pm Sat & Sun

Live music and draft beer make the deck at Angel Island Café a good place to hang out on weekends. Catch the ferry from Sausalito (see website for details) and head for the picnic tables on the lawns around Ayala Cove where sailboats, kayaks, and power yachts come and go. Walking and biking trails connect historic sites and a secluded beach.

4 Cliff's Variety
MAP E5 ▪ 479 Castro St ▪ (415) 431-5365 ▪ Open 9am–8pm Mon–Fri, 9:30am–8pm Sat, 11am–6pm Sun ▪ www.cliffsvariety.com

Since 1936, this store in the heart of the Castro has been an emporium of hardware, quirky decor and kitchen utensils, toys, old-fashioned candy, and surprises. Local gay residents come for costumes, wigs, tiaras, and boas; tourists come for souvenirs and people-watching.

The SS *Jeremiah O'Brien* Liberty Ship

5 SS Jeremiah O'Brien
MAP F1 ▪ Pier 45 ▪ (415) 441-3101 ▪ Open 9am–4pm daily ▪ www.ssjeremiahobrien.org

Ferrying troops and supplies during World War II, 441-ft- (134-m-) long SS *Jeremiah O'Brien* was part of the invasion of Normandy, and is one of only two restored survivors of the original 2,710 Liberty Ships. She fires up her engines on "Steaming Weekends" and there are daily tours.

6 Letterman Digital Arts Center

MAP D2 ■ Letterman Drive ■ (415) 746-5444 ■ Open 9am–5pm Mon–Fri ■ www.lucasfilm.com

On the east end of the Presidio, at the headquarters of Lucasfilm, Yoda tops a fountain and in the lobby you can see the Darth Vader costume and other *Star Wars* artifacts. Rest from the excitement in the lovely landscaped public park with views toward the Golden Gate Bridge.

7 Gospel Music at Glide Memorial Church

Crowds gather every Sunday at 9am and 11am for the joyful noise of services at Glide Memorial United Methodist Church. With a 125-voice gospel choir singing jazz, blues, and rock and roll, plus an audience made up of all ages, races, and religions, the emotional scene is set for the flamboyant Reverend Cecil Williams, who welcomes all comers *(see p48)*.

8 Yachting and Bowling in the Park

MAP B4 ■ Golden Gate Park ■ (415) 386-1037 ■ Open 1–4pm daily & for special events ■ www.sfmyc.org ■ www.sflbc.org

For more than a century, the members of the Lawn Bowling Club, clad all in white, have welcomed spectators at their greensward. The steam-powered and electric sailing vessels of the Model Yacht Club can be seen zooming across Spreckels Lake daily, and during the Wooden Boats on Parade event held every second year in October.

Lawn Bowling Club, Golden Gate Park

9 Cottage Row

MAP F3 ■ Between Sutter & Bush ■ (415) 391-2000 ■ Open sunrise–sunset

The hidden gem of Cottage Row Historic District is lined with late 1800s Italianate houses from the days of horse-drawn streetcars. Around the corner are "Painted Ladies" – elaborate Victorian houses.

10 Presidio Sculptures

MAP D2 ■ www.presidio.gov

Sculptures by Andy Goldsworthy are set in the Presidio forest. His 100-ft (30-m) *Spire*, made of cypress trees, towers in a copse. *Wood Line* is in century-old eucalyptus groves.

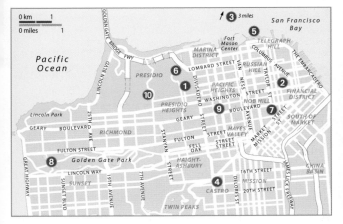

🔟 Day Trips from the City

Giant redwoods in Muir Woods

① Muir Woods
Muir Woods National Monument ▪ (415) 388-2595 ▪ Open 8am–sunset daily ▪ Adm ▪ www.nps.gov/muwo

At the foot of Mount Tamalpais (see p126), this 550-acre (222-ha) woodland is home to one of the few remaining first-growth groves of redwoods. The oldest of these giants is at least 1,000 years old. Such trees once covered the coastal area of California. The woods are named in honor of John Muir, the 19th-century conservationist (see p47).

② Big Basin Redwoods State Park
Highway 9 is one of the most picturesque drives in the Bay Area, winding its way among green mountains and through little towns on the way to this park, which, although it's a relatively short drive from Silicon Valley, has a backwoods feel.

③ Saratoga and Los Gatos
Hakone Gardens: 21000 Big Basin Way, Saratoga ▪ (408) 741-4994 ▪ Open 10am–5pm Mon–Fri, 11am–5pm Sat–Sun ▪ Adm ▪ www.hakone.com

Both of these towns, situated in the hills above Silicon Valley, have retained their frontier quality (see p129). One of the best things to do, other than drive the scenic roads, is to visit Hakone Gardens, a beautiful Japanese park.

④ Monterey Peninsula
Day-trippers head to Monterey for its world-class aquarium, to shop and eat on Cannery Row (made famous by John Steinbeck), and to ramble along the shores of Point Lobos State Natural Reserve. Carmel-by-the-Sea is full of quaint cottages, art galleries, and boutique shops, as well as having a picturesque beach. Golfers make pilgrimages to see legendary Pebble Beach and Spanish Bay golf clubs, and to play at Bayonet Black Horse and Pacific Grove courses.

Big Basin Redwoods State Park offers creek and forest environments

5 The Wine Country

Taking at least a day to drive up into the Napa and Sonoma valleys should be on everyone's San Francisco to-do list. Not only is the countryside beautiful, but also you can sample some of the best wines in the world. Dip into the restorative volcanic hot springs, and enjoy lavish spa treatments (see pp36–9).

6 Stanford University

Located just 30 minutes south of the city, with a Caltrain depot right at the main gates, the palm-lined beauty of this campus makes it worth a trip (see p126). The visual motif of sandstone and red-tile roofs has been carried forward since the Romanesque Quadrangle was built in the late 1800s. The ornate carvings that decorate the arches and pillars are extraordinarily lovely, setting off the elaborate mosaic that graces the facade of the Memorial Church.

7 Half Moon Bay

This charming Victorian-era town is fringed with long, sandy beaches that are perfect for strolling and surfing. Half Moon Bay State Beach is actually made up of 3 miles (5 km) of adjacent beaches, alongside which the Coastside Trail runs. The local flower farms and busy fishing port are photogenic, with fresh seafood, art galleries, and country stores add to the mix.

8 Santa Cruz

This beach resort has always had a reputation for the vibrancy of its countercultural way of life. Along the beautiful coastline, the most prominent feature is the boardwalk's Giant Dipper Roller Coaster, which has been thrilling Santa Cruzers since 1923. The best swimming in the Bay Area is also here (see p129).

9 Point Reyes

Some 110 sq miles (285 sq km) of pristine natural coastline make this promontory a haven for all sorts of wildlife and a thing of unforgettable, windswept beauty. You can watch whales and sea lions from Point Reyes Lighthouse (see p129).

Point Reyes Lighthouse

10 Sonoma Coast

The Tides Wharf: 835 Coast Highway One ■ (707) 875-3652

About an hour's scenic drive from the city rewards with sandy beaches, rocky coves, and the fisherman's village of Bodega Bay. From the deck or a window table at the Tides Wharf seafood restaurant, watch harbor seals play and fishermen unload their catches, then take a drive along world-famous Highway 1, stopping off at Sonoma Coast beaches.

🔟 Children's Attractions

Children's Creativity Museum, Yerba Buena Gardens

1 Children's Creativity Museum

This elaborate complex, aimed both at entertaining kids and spurring their creativity to the max, is part of the greater Yerba Buena Gardens. There's an old-fashioned carousel; a labyrinth; a studio where they can script, produce, and star in their own videos; art studios; and a digital workshop, plus lots more to keep them busy all day long. Suitable for those aged 5 to 18 (see p32).

2 San Francisco Zoo

Direct encounters with farm animals and visits with zoo babies, which may include gorillas, snow leopards, rhinos, or alpacas, make this a must-do for the youngsters. Although perhaps not the biggest or best zoo in the world, its attention to top-quality children's programs, such as the many feeding times and the creepy-crawly insect denizens, make it one of the best for budding zoologists. The landscaping of the whole place, from the carousel to the natural habitats, is also designed for maximum fun (see p119).

3 Aquariums

Part of Golden Gate Park's California Academy of Sciences (see pp26–7), the Steinhart Aquarium is a big hit with kids. The darkened corridors are filled with softly glowing tanks in which some of the weirdest creatures on the planet disport themselves. Then there's the Touching Tidal Pool if kids want to get up close and personal with their finny friends. At Fisherman's Wharf, Aquarium of the Bay gives an even greater undersea experience, with walk-through transparent tunnels surrounded by sea life (see p16).

4 Randall Museum

MAP E4 ■ 199 Museum Way, off Roosevelt Way, Buena Vista ■ (415) 554-9600 ■ Open 10am–5pm Tue–Sat ■ www.randallmuseum.org

Perched above the city, in Corona Heights Park, this small, welcoming complex is primarily a petting zoo, with farm animals, raccoons, reptiles, and birds. But it also offers hands-on experiences, with woodworking, pottery, painting, theater, photography, model railroads, storytelling, gardening, and more. The aim of the museum is to teach children respect for nature and the environment.

5 Alcatraz

"The Rock" is always a hit with older children, particularly those who enjoy the grim, quasi-military aspects of the place. The wildness of the island's natural beauty, as well as the ferry ride out and back, will also delight. Smaller kids may find it a bit frightening *(see pp18–21)*.

6 Bay Area Discovery Museum

557 McReynolds Rd, Sausalito ■ **(415) 339-3900** ■ **Open 9am–4pm Tue–Fri, 10am–5pm Sat–Sun** ■ **Closed public hols & last two weeks in Sep** ■ **Dis. access** ■ **Adm** ■ **www.baykidsmuseum.org**

This hands-on museum is aimed directly at entertaining children. Kids will be able to enjoy an art studio, a science lab, a wave workshop where they learn about sea and plant life, and a media center.

7 Exploratorium

Kids can experience one of the finest San Francisco interactive days at this superb science museum at Pier 15. They'll learn all about their senses and how they work, as well as delve into all the laws of physics through first-hand experiments, like making simple circuit boards. The top draw, however, is the Tactile Dome, a dark sphere in which you feel your way along, touching a range of sensorially stimulating objects and textures *(see p88)*.

Making circuit boards, Exploratorium

8 Golden Gate Park Playground

At the southeastern corner of the park, kids will love the old carousel, a treehouse, and some great swings,

slides, and other kid-orientated rides. In the summer, there are often Punch and Judy shows to delight children of all ages *(see pp24–5)*.

Angel Island State Park

9 Angel Island State Park

Angel Island is an ideal place for a full-day family outing. You can picnic, swim, hike, kayak, camp, or take the tram tour that goes all around the island, with a guide who points out sites of historic interest – dating from the days when the place was a rather forbidding immigrant clearing station *(see p96)*.

10 Metreon

Intended as a bustling, high-tech, multilevel amusement arcade for adolescents, so far the only thing that seems to have clicked is the superb multiscreen cinema complex. Here you can watch the latest Hollywood blockbusters and chart-toppers with full digital sound effects amped up to the highest possible level. Otherwise, the Metreon offers several different restaurant choices and great views over the city from the fourth-floor deck space *(see p32)*.

🔟 Performing Arts Venues

War Memorial Opera House and San Francisco Ballet

1 War Memorial Opera House and San Francisco Ballet
MAP R1 ▪ 301 Van Ness Ave ▪ (415) 864-3330

The San Francisco Opera Company is the second largest in the country and performs here from June to January. The excellent San Francisco Ballet, one of the nation's oldest ballet companies, mostly performs at the War Memorial Opera House.

2 Louise M. Davies Symphony Hall
MAP R1 ▪ 201 Van Ness Ave ▪ (415) 864-6000

With performances from September through to May, under the directorship of Michael Tilson Thomas, the San Francisco Symphony Orchestra performs in this modern structure with its carefully modulated acoustics. Built in 1980, this curving, glass-fronted concert hall is loved and loathed in equal measure by locals. Its corner placement is set off by a Henry Moore bronze sculpture, which has also had its fair share of detractors.

3 Masonic Auditorium
MAP N3 ▪ 1111 California St ▪ (415) 776-7457

Originally a Masonic Temple, built in 1957, this attractive structure, with its 3,000-seat auditorium, is used as a venue for jazz performances, lectures, and readings, as well as conventions and seminars. Mosaics inside and out depict some of the tenets of Freemasonry.

4 Curran Theater
MAP P3 ▪ 445 Geary St ▪ (415) 551-2000 ▪ www.shnsf.com

Built in 1922, this is one of the grandest theaters in the city and a Registered National Historic Landmark. The interior is a fantasy of gold and carved wood, complemented by a vast chandelier and murals. Shows tend toward long-running Broadway hits.

5 Beach Blanket Babylon
MAP L4 ▪ Club Fugazi, 678 Green St ▪ (415) 421-4222

High camp and high headdresses, along with jolly good singing by the veteran ensemble cast, make this one of the joys of the city. It's been zinging the heartstrings of lovers of

Singer, Beach Blanket Babylon

San Francisco for more than a quarter of a century and shows no signs of flagging. The excuse for all this frivolity is the sending up of various notables, most of whom well deserve the good-natured ribbing.

6 Orpheum Theatre
MAP R2 ▪ 1192 Market St ▪ (415) 551-2000 ▪ www.shnsf.com

Originally a vaudeville house and then a movie theater, this is the historic spot where *Hair* was given its first West Coast performance some 30 years ago – known locally as "the New York version of what happened here in San Francisco." The theater, decorated in 1920s Moorish style, now mostly stages Broadway shows.

Orpheum Theatre

7 SFJAZZ Center
MAP R1 ▪ 205 Franklin St at Fell St ▪ (866) 920-5299

With specially designed acoustics and an intimate concert hall, the luminous building that houses the SFJAZZ Center is the first in the US to be specifically built for jazz performances. The center aims to educate and inspire audiences with an eclectic program of events from world-class musicians.

8 Golden Gate Theater
MAP Q3 ▪ 1 Taylor St ▪ (415) 551-2000 ▪ www.shnsf.com

This former movie house, designed with Moorish influences in the 1920s, is one of the city's larger mainstream theaters. Its usual offerings are traveling Broadway blockbusters, such as *Wicked*, *West Side Story*, and Monty Python's *Spamalot*.

9 American Conservatory Theater (ACT)
MAP P3 ▪ Geary Theater, 415 Geary St ▪ (415) 749-2228 ▪ www.act-sf.org

Founded in the 1960s, San Francisco's most important theater company is internationally respected and has produced premieres of a number of major plays. At the heart of ACT is one of the most acclaimed actor-training institutions in the nation – former students include Annette Bening and Winona Ryder.

10 Magic Theatre
MAP F1 ▪ Fort Mason Center, Bldg D ▪ (415) 441-8822 ▪ www.magictheatre.org

In the 1970s, none other than Sam Shepard was the resident playwright of the Magic, and its stage has seen performances by the likes of Sean Penn and Nick Nolte. It specializes in new plays, usually by up-and-coming Americans and also offers "raw play" readings of as yet unstaged works.

𝗧𝗢𝗣 𝟭𝟬 Nightlife

The Tonga Room and Hurricane Bar offer a South Sea Island theme

1 The Tonga Room and Hurricane Bar

MAP N3 ■ **Fairmont Hotel, 950 Mason St** ■ **(415) 772-5278**

This Nob Hill tiki bar is almost Disneyesque in its tropical effects, including indoor monsoons and a floating band. Aimed at grown-ups of every age, it has delivered kitschy Polynesian dazzlement since 1945, and is often chosen as the venue for birthday celebrations. The bar's award-winning weekday happy hour (5–7pm) includes an Asian buffet at nominal cost.

2 Mighty

One of the few San Francisco venues large enough to be considered a proper dance club, Mighty is well known for hip-hop shows and international house DJs. It is beloved by club-goers for its great variety of music, its size, and its revolving art collection (see p113).

3 Mezzanine

Located in the SoMa district, industrial-chic Mezzanine comprises one large room with a long bar and a concrete dance floor. Mezzanine hosts live music from touring indie bands, esoteric hip-hop acts, and visiting DJs, such as Juan Maclean and the Three 6 Mafia (see p114).

4 Bottom of the Hill

Open seven days a week in Potrero Hill, this is one of the best live-music venues in a city renowned for its live music. Even though Bottom of the Hill has a definite punk vibe, you are just as likely to hear a folk music act playing as a hard-core punk band. If you don't care for the music, just head to the back where you can grab a table out of earshot (see p114).

5 Harry Denton's Starlight Room

MAP P4 ■ **Sir Francis Drake Hotel, 450 Powell St at Sutter** ■ **(415) 395-8595**

Something for the 40-plus set, or even 50-plus, and those who enjoy dancing, good views, and great cocktails. Twenty-one stories above

Harry Denton's Starlight Room

Union Square, couples can dance to jazz and the milder R&B hits, and relax in the easy sophistication of this place. The theme is 1930s-stylish, so consider it a chance to dress up in smart suits and party dresses, sip highballs, and enjoy the city's seductive lights.

6 Bimbo's 365 Club
MAP K3 ■ 1025 Columbus Ave ■ (415) 474-0365

Whether you are into swing, jazz, rock, or grunge, this San Francisco institution delivers. A retro-chic yet unpretentious music venue since 1931, this hopping bar with glittering decor and an old-school feel brings in all the top acts.

7 Supperclub
Changes venue every 3–6 months ■ (415) 348-0900 ■ www.supperclub-sf.com

If ultra-chic surroundings are what you are looking for, then this is the club for you – San Francisco at its trendiest. It attracts a young and sexy crowd. Whether you are after dancing or highly original perform-ances, this is the place. The pricey cover charge is worth it.

8 Great American Music Hall
MAP P1 ■ 859 O'Farrell St ■ (415) 885-0750 ■ www.gamh.com

With a colorful history, the Great American Music Hall is now a cool spot to see live music, including indie rock, country, folk, jazz, and blues. The views from the tables around the Victorian balcony are excellent and the sound quality is top-notch. Downstairs is standing room. Food and drinks are available.

9 Le Colonial
People flock here for the cuisine, the live music, or to sit in the

Deck furniture at Le Colonial

lounge for tea or cocktails. Live swing, jazz, and blues bands entertain guests from Monday to Thursday, including the very popular Martini Brothers Band. Head to the club upstairs on Friday and Saturday nights as the DJ spins house tracks to a crowded dance floor from 9:30pm to 2am. Situated just off Union Square, the location doesn't get much better (see p94).

10 Punchline Comedy Club
MAP M5 ■ 444 Battery St ■ (415) 397-7573

A perfect alternative to bar-hopping, there is no better venue for a good laugh than this hilarious comedy club. National acts (and local ones too) headline a fun evening in an intimate setting, with all the seating up close to the stage. It's best to buy tickets in advance to ensure seating.

TOP 10 Gay and Lesbian Venues

1 Moby Dick
MAP E5 ■ 4049 18th St ■ (415) 861-1199 ■ www.mobydicksf.com

This old-time Castro hangout attracts a more mature crowd. It's generally a bunch of regulars getting together for pinball or pool. The windows are big, so you can keep track of what's going down on the street. The music is largely 1980s retro, which sets a fun-loving tone.

2 Eagle SF
MAP G4 ■ 398 12th St

Bikers and leather boys still rule at this venerable SoMa dive. Come here to revel in the beer-busting, testosterone-filled atmosphere. The back patio gets going on Sunday afternoons, and Thursdays feature performances by local bands.

3 The Lion Pub
MAP E3 ■ 2062 Divisadero St at Sacramento ■ (415) 567-6565

The city's oldest gay bar is also its most upscale. It attracts the more yuppified denizens of the gay community who appreciate the stylish renovated Victorian setting in which it is housed. There's interesting music, excellent cocktails, a great fireplace, free food at happy hour, and hobnobbing with a wealthier clientele.

4 Harvey's
MAP E5 ■ 500 Castro St at 18th ■ (415) 431-4278

Named in honor of the slain gay politician Harvey Milk (see p47), this is the ideal place to get to know the look and feel of the Castro district. There's lots of gay memorabilia on the walls, the staff are friendly, the ambience easygoing, and not at all

Fun-loving Moby Dick

quirky or kinky. It's the more wholesome face of gay San Francisco. Happy hour lasts from 3 to 7pm on weekdays only.

5 Martuni's
MAP F4 ■ 4 Valencia St at Market ■ (415) 241-0205

With its decor of glass and chrome and the regulars' penchant for singing old torch songs, this is a very retro piano bar for an older gay crowd. It's a magnet for butch guys, drag queens, and straights, too – anyone who likes a good singalong – or who doesn't mind embarrassing themselves on the microphone.

6 Badlands
MAP E5 ■ 4121 18th St ■ (415) 626-9320

Its old, dingy interior used to live up to its menacing name, but no more since it has gone all slick and shiny. Still, it's a big draw for the under-40 set. The Sunday afternoon beer bust (4–9pm) is, for many, the most happening event of the week.

Neon sign outside Twin Peaks

7 Twin Peaks
MAP E5 ■ 401 Castro St ■ (415) 864-9470

Conveniently located on the corner of Market Street, this legendary and distinctive tavern offers one of the best views of the Castro, whether by day or night. The interior is an inviting, pillowed triangular space with plate-glass windows.

Interior of The Midnight Sun

8 The Midnight Sun
MAP E5 ■ 4067 18th St ■ (415) 861-4186

This popular, posy video bar fills up quickly after office hours and stays that way until the wee hours. Mostly frequented by good-looking 20- and 30-somethings, it's more about being admired than making connections here, so it's best to go with a friend or two, have a drink, and then move on to some livelier venue. The video screens show a mix of music clips and TV sitcoms. Drinks are two for one until 9pm every day of the week.

9 Lush Lounge
MAP F3 ■ 1221 Polk St at Fern ■ (415) 771-2022

It's hard not to have a great time at this lively little piano bar in Polk Gulch. Frequented by the local transvestite community, as well as straight office workers from the surrounding neighborhood, Lush Lounge is always an experience. Happy hour runs until 7pm daily.

10 Lexington Club
MAP F5 ■ 3464 19th St at Valencia ■ (415) 863-2052

The only full-time "girl" bar in the city, set in a Mission District neighborhood that has been on the rise as a lesbian enclave. Young, pierced sylphs, 40-something professionals, and even straight women frequent this fun "down-home, divey den for dykes," as one devotee dubbed it.

ᴛᴏᴘ10 Restaurants

Intimate and modern interior at two-Michelin-starred Quince

① Quince
Run by Michelin-starred chef Michael Tusk, Quince is considered by many to be the best restaurant in the city. It serves dish after dish of beautiful Californian fare, influenced by northern Italy and made with the freshest local ingredients *(see p95)*.

② Gitane
Worth a visit as much for its dramatic, gypsy bordello atmosphere as for its delicious Iberian entrées. Drawing on the rich cuisines of Portugal, Morocco, southern Spain, and France, Gitane offers mouth-watering tagines as well as lamb, pork, and fish dishes, all of which are served with considerable flair and lots of flavor *(see p95)*.

③ La Mar
Surprisingly, La Mar is one of San Francisco's few top-notch seafood restaurants. It serves wonderful, super-fresh Peruvian seafood (including an astounding assortment of tasty *ceviches*) in a stunning blue and white dining room looking out over the Bay *(see p95)*.

④ A16
Known for its authentic Neapolitan pizzas, fresh pastas, house-cured salami, and regional wines, this casual yet chic marina restaurant will transport you straight to southern Italy *(see p101)*.

⑤ Greens
The first fine-dining vegetarian restaurant in the city, it was originally inspired by the huge success of the Zen bakery and coffee shop. This spacious, pleasant Marina restaurant came to define vegetarian cuisine for the entire Bay Area *(see p101)*.

⑥ Nopalito
MAP H3 ▪ 306 Broderick St at Oak ▪ (415) 437-0303 ▪ Dis. access ▪ $
From the folks at Nopa *(see p107)* comes a fresh take on Mexican fare. Nopalito focuses on traditional Mexican street food – including *carnitas* and *taquitos*. The cocktails are just as fantastic as the food itself, but be prepared to wait.

⑦ Foreign Cinema
MAP F5 ▪ 2534 Mission St ▪ (415) 648-7600 ▪ Dis. access ▪ $$
In the courtyard, a selection of old and new movies are projected onto a neighboring building while you dine. The Mediterranean-influenced food is also excellent and the oyster bar and Sunday brunch are popular.

8 Lers Ros Thai

MAP K2 ■ 730 Larkin St ■ (415) 931-6917 ■ Dis. access ■ $

Lers Ros delivers authentic Thai dishes in a no-frills, casual dining room. Arrive early or you'll be standing in line down the street. Reservations are also available.

9 Delfina

Thanks to its perfect, modern Italian fare made with the freshest local ingredients, it has been hard to get a table at Delfina for years now, which is saying a lot in a city that has trendy restaurants opening every month. In addition to the legendary chicken and delicate pasta dishes at Delfina, you can indulge in the best Neapolitan pizza outside of Italy at its pizzeria next door *(see p115)*.

10 Spruce

MAP D3 ■ 3640 Sacramento St ■ (415) 931-5100 ■ Closed L ■ Dis. access ■ $$$

This restaurant's excellent seasonal Nouveau American menu has a major meat focus. For the same delicious food with a slightly less formal feel, opt to sit in the bar.

Pastrami sandwich, Spruce

TOP 10 ROMANTIC DINNER SPOTS

Cliff House

1 Atelier Crenn
MAP E2 ■ 3127 Fillmore ■ (415) 440-0460 ■ Dis. access ■ $$$
Delicious food, and the dining room is intimate and quiet.

2 Cliff House
A wild setting with views of crashing waves *(see p123)*.

3 Acquerello
MAP N1 ■ 1722 Sacramento St ■ (415) 567-5432 ■ $$$
The black truffles are an aphrodisiac.

4 Masa's Restaurant
MAP N4 ■ 648 Bush St ■ (415) 989-7154 ■ $$$
French cuisine in elegant surroundings.

5 Boulevard
MAP H2 ■ 1 Mission St ■ (415) 543-6084 ■ $$$
Belle époque decor and superb food.

6 Chez Spencer
MAP G4 ■ 82 14th St ■ (415) 864-2191 ■ Dis. access ■ $$
French fare in a fairy-lit garden.

7 Aziza
MAP C3 ■ 5800 Geary Blvd ■ (415) 752-2222 ■ Dis. access ■ $$$
Delicious, Michelin-starred cuisine.

8 Gary Danko
MAP K2 ■ 800 N Point St ■ (415) 749-2060 ■ Dis. access ■ $$$
Sophisticated contemporary cuisine.

9 Frascati
MAP L2 ■ 1901 Hyde St ■ (415) 928-1406 ■ Dis. access ■ $$
Italian fare and great views.

10 Chez Panisse
1517 Shattuck Ave, Berkeley, off Hwy 80 ■ (510) 548-5525 ■ Dis. access ■ $$$
The birthplace of Cal-Med cuisine. Book weeks ahead.

For a key to restaurant price ranges see p95

TOP 10 Cafés and Bars

1 The Buena Vista Café
Opened in 1916 at the cable car turnaround at Fisherman's Wharf, this friendly bar and eatery claims to have been the first to introduce Irish coffee to America in 1952. First served at Shannon Airport in Ireland, the drink is composed of Irish whiskey, a sugar cube, hot coffee, and a foamy collar of whipped cream *(see p101)*.

2 Caffè Trieste
A North Beach landmark that must be experienced if you have any interest whatsoever in the colorful history of this quarter – whether it is from the literary and artistic point of view, or for the Italian culture. It's a great place for a cup of whatever warm liquid you favor, and to sit and people-watch, or dip into one of San Francisco's free weekly newspapers *(see p94)*.

3 Blue Bottle Café
This hip coffee roaster kicked off San Francisco's latest café trend; it serves up perfect cappuccinos and lattes in its chic, industrial SoMa space. Also on offer are Kyoto-style iced coffees, brewed using the Japanese slow-drip method. Perfection takes time, however, and these baristas take their work very seriously, so be prepared for a bit of a wait. The experience is worth trying at least once *(see p94)*.

Slow-drip brewers, Blue Bottle Café

Fresh bread, Tartine Bakery and Café

4 Tartine Bakery and Café
MAP F5 ■ 600 Guerrero St ■ (415) 487-1600
You may find a line out the door at this purveyor of rustic breads, "hot pressed" sandwiches, pizzas, cakes, and tarts. The co-owners have both been awarded the James Beard Award for Outstanding Pastry Chefs.

5 Réveille Coffee Co.
MAP E5 ■ 4076 18th St ■ (415) 789-6258
Coffee aficionados gather at this neighborhood café in the Castro (also with branches in North Beach and Jackson Square) for meticulously crafted espresso drinks. Watch the buzzing street from the patio as you enjoy home-made granola, tasty sandwiches, or savory flatbreads.

6 Tosca
MAP M4 ■ 242 Columbus Ave ■ (415) 986-9651 ■ Dis. access
With Sean Penn and Kid Rock as owners of this bar, you can celebrity-spot as you sip potent cocktails and listen to opera on the jukebox.

7 Dolores Park Café
MAP F5 ■ 501 Dolores St ■ (415) 621-2936 ■ Dis. access
This funky neighborhood café has it all – views of Dolores Park, filling

breakfast and lunch fare, home-made smoothies, freshly baked pastries, and live music and spoken word performances on Friday nights.

8 Bourbon & Branch
MAP P3 ■ 501 Jones St at O'Farrell ■ (415) 346-1735
You'll need the nightly password to enter this bar. Once inside, enjoy inventive cocktails in one of the most beautifully designed bars in the city, and explore more secret rooms.

9 Vesuvio
MAP M4 ■ 255 Columbus Ave ■ (415) 362-3370
Since 1948 Vesuvio has been the North Beach haunt of artists, writers, and bon vivants of all stripes, many of whom wander across the street to the famous City Lights Bookstore *(see p92)* and back.

10 Smuggler's Cove
MAP F3 ■ 650 Gough St ■ (415) 869-1900
The quirky pirate-ship decor creates a fun setting for this three-level tiki bar with a menu of rums, Caribbean cocktails, and classic libations from Prohibition-era Havana.

Selection of rum at Smuggler's Cove

TOP 10 BRUNCH VENUES

French toast

1 Dottie's True Blue Café
MAP G3 ■ 28 6th St ■ Closed Tue, Wed ■ Dis. access
It's a SoMa tradition to stand in line for the American breakfasts.

2 Sears Fine Food
A Union Square institution, noted for its silver dollar pancakes *(see p95)*.

3 Ella's
MAP E3 ■ 500 Presidio Ave ■ Dis. access
Expect to wait at this breakfast haven.

4 Mama's on Washington Square
MAP L4 ■ 1701 Stockton St ■ Closed Mon ■ Dis. access
The greatest French toast in town.

5 Sparky's Diner
MAP F4 ■ 242 Church St at Market
Omelets and hash browns draw crowds to this popular 24-hour diner.

6 Presidio Social Club
MAP E2 ■ 563 Ruger St ■ Dis. access
An elegant restaurant serving up old-school drinks and brunch classics.

7 Just for You
MAP H5 ■ 732 22nd St ■ Dis. access
Soul food-inspired brunch in the Dogpatch neighborhood.

8 Kate's Kitchen
MAP F4 ■ 471 Haight St ■ Dis. access
Huge portions of breakfast specialties, including a "French Toast Orgy."

9 Chloe's Café
MAP F6 ■ 1399 Church St at 26th
Banana or pecan pancakes, and cinnamon French toast.

10 Red Door Café
MAP F3 ■ 1608 Bush St
This café is as beloved for its comical owner as for its fluffy omelets and perfect French toast.

🔟 Stores and Shopping Center

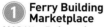
Ferry Building Marketplace

① Ferry Building Marketplace
MAP H2 ■ Embarcadero at Market
Feast on specialties from around the Bay and take home regional chocolates and olive oil.

② Nordstrom
MAP Q4 ■ Westfield San Francisco Center, 865 Market St
Located on the top five floors of the Westfield Center, the fashion emporium is known as the "store in the sky." Impeccable service, a vast selection, and a refined atmosphere featuring live piano music make this a very upscale shopping experience.

③ Neiman Marcus
MAP P4 ■ 150 Stockton St
This high-end store overlooks Union Square from a plum spot once occupied by the City of Paris building, which was constructed in the 1890s but torn down to build this modern structure. Part of the original building remains, however, by way of the huge stained-glass dome. Neiman's boast is that it can get anything you might want. Lunch in the rotunda is the least expensive way to experience the store.

④ Gump's
MAP P4 ■ 135 Post St
Founded in 1861 by German immigrants, this homegrown department store has one of the largest collections in the US of fine china and crystal, selling famous names such as Baccarat, Lalique, and Georg Jensen silver. For more designer options continue down Post Street to Crocker Galleria.

⑤ Macy's
MAP P4 ■ 170 O'Farrell St
This old-guard department store has become an all-purpose emporium carrying merchandise in all price ranges. During the Christmas holidays, the window displays are well worth a look.

⑥ Barney's New York
MAP G3 ■ 77 O'Farrell St
This store comprises four full stories of style in Union Square. It's the place to go for both men and women to find those must-have designer clothes, shoes, and accessories from the likes of Marc Jacobs and Comme des Garçons. It also boasts the best fragrance department in the city. Just be prepared to pay handsomely for all those clothes.

⑦ Saks Fifth Avenue
MAP P4 ■ 384 Post St
For decades, the name Saks has been synonymous with high style, and this branch of the New York mainstay is one of the best embodiments of the store's mythic élan. You'll find just about every international designer of note here.

Saks Fifth Avenue

⑧ Embarcadero Center
MAP N6 ■ Embarcadero & Battery, Sacramento & Clay Sts

Four high-rise blocks connect to form this sprawling shopping center. Dominated by chain stores such as Gap, it's probably not the best place to find a unique souvenir. The upper floors host restaurants and a movie theater.

Ghirardelli Square, Fisherman's Wharf

⑨ Ghirardelli Square
MAP K1 ■ 900 North Point St

Housing over 20 restaurants and shops, this former chocolate factory has become one of the most frequented destinations in Fisherman's Wharf. The stores range from tourist T-shirt shops to fine jewelry boutiques (see p16).

⑩ Westfield Shopping Center
MAP Q4 ■ 865 Market St

This huge center has ten levels and nearly 400 stores, including Bloomingdale's, a movie theater, and a gourmet food area.

TOP 10 SHOPPING AREAS

Grant Avenue

1 Union Square
Traditionally the focal point of all the best stores, including Tiffany & Co, Armani, Prada, Cartier, Yves St Laurent, Chanel, and more (see p89).

2 Union Street
Converted Victorian homes house a charming assortment of boutiques, bookstores, antiques shops, restaurants, and a cinema (see p103).

3 Grant Avenue
MAP N4
Chic shopping off Union Square, exotic Chinatown emporiums, and North Beach hangouts in Upper Grant.

4 Upper Fillmore Street
MAP E2
A colorful choice of cafés, restaurants, and boutiques, all geared to a high-end Pacific Heights clientele.

5 Market Street
MAP Q3
A good place to find cut-rate electronics and outlet stores, as well as the Westfield Shopping Center.

6 Hayes Valley
These blocks offer galleries and stores with an avant-garde feel (see p105).

7 Chestnut Street
MAP K1
Clothing boutiques, health-food shops, and an old-fashioned cinema.

8 The Mission
Plenty of discount stores and funky home furnishing shops (see p111).

9 Castro Street
Fine shops, gay bookstores and erotic boutiques (see p109).

10 Haight Street
The place for secondhand clothing, emporiums, and shoe stores (see p105).

TOP 10 San Francisco for Free

The Music Concourse, Golden Gate Park

1 Outdoor Summer Concerts

Sigmund Stern Grove at 19th Ave & Sloat Blvd ▪ (415) 252-6252 ▪ Jun–Aug: Sun ▪ www.sterngrove.org

Pines and eucalyptus create a verdant backdrop for the grassy amphitheater where the Stern Grove Festival free concerts take place on summer Sundays. Thousands picnic while enjoying jazz, rock, the symphony, ballet, and opera.

2 Waterfront Ramble

The Wave Organ: MAP E1 ▪ 83 Marina Green Drive

There is a lot to enjoy for free along the waterfront. Listen to *The Wave Organ*, an acoustic wave-activated sculpture, peruse murals in the Maritime Museum *(see p53)*, stroll the Hyde Street Pier past the 1886 square-rigged ship *Balcutha*, watch sea lions at Pier 39, or bask in the misty *Fog Bridge* installation at the Exploratorium *(see p88)*.

3 Bayside View of the San Francisco Giants

MAP H3 ▪ Giants Promenade

During baseball season it's free to watch the San Francisco Giants play at home in the AT&T Park from the Giants Promenade walkway.

4 Golden Gate Park

Opera in the Park: www.sfopera.com

This 1,000-acre (405-ha) urban garden is a great place to watch tai chi classes, swing dancing, or bison roaming in their paddock. The Music Concourse hosts free concerts in summer, including the annual Opera in the Park event *(see pp24–5)*.

5 Fort Point National Historic Site

Situated at the foot of the Golden Gate Bridge, this fortress was built in 1861 to protect the city of San Francisco from Confederate attacks that never came. Children in particular love to see the cannons being loaded, as well as the Civil War reenactments *(see p47)*.

Cannon at Fort Point

6 Guided Walking Tours
(415) 557-4266 ▪ www.
sfcityguides.org
Dozens of daily, free walking tours
are led by savvy locals and
historians, giving insights into Coit
Tower murals, Chinatown alleys, the
gay Castro, Victorian architecture,
the Gold Rush, and other topics.

7 City Hall
Wander through the 1915
Beaux Arts City Hall, situated in the
Civic Center (see p89), which houses
city government and public art. Tour
guides tell of glory days and trag-
edies, such as the 1906 earthquake
and the assassination of Mayor
George Moscone in 1978 (see p43).

8 Free Museum Days
The first Tuesday of every
month, museums open their doors
for free, including the de Young
Museum (see pp28–9), the European-
art-filled Legion of Honor (see p52),
contemporary-focused Yerba Buena
Center for the Arts (see p32), and the
San Francisco Museum of Craft and
Design (see p53). Set in a stunning
Beaux Arts edifice, the Asian Art
Museum is free on the first Sunday
of the month (see pp52–3).

9 The Presidio
The Officers' Club:
www.presidioofficersclub.com
Take a ranger-led tour to experience
200 years of military history, from
Spanish cannons to Civil War
barracks. The Officers' Club also
runs free cultural events. Meander
the forest trails and enjoy a picnic
on the beach or in the seaview
meadows (see pp98–9).

10 Golden Gate Bridge
Whether under cloudy or
sunny skies, a walk or cycle across
the "international orange" Golden
Gate Bridge is a must. The iconic
symbol of the city towers 260 ft
(79 m) above churning Bay waters,
and offers spectacular views of
Alcatraz Island, sailboats, freighters,
and ferries (see pp12–13).

TOP 10 MONEY-SAVING TIPS

Hardly Strictly Bluegrass festival

1 Self-cater and picnic with locally
sourced food from the city's
world-famous farmers' markets.
www.cafarmersmkts.com

2 Go San Francisco Card holders get
free and discounted admission to more
than 25 attractions, tours, and cruises.
www.gosanfranciscocard.com

3 Print out the current SF Travel
Coupons for discounted cruises, tours,
attractions, shopping, and more.
www.sftravelcoupons.com

4 Tix Bay Area sells half-price tickets to
cultural events, both online and at the
booth on Union Square.
www.tixbayarea.org

5 One of the largest multi-genre music
festivals in the country, 3-day Hardly
Strictly Bluegrass is free to all.
www.hardlystrictlybluegrass.com

6 Happy-hour bar menus of small
plates and discounted drinks are
available from about 4pm to 7pm.

7 Discount coupons and special offers
are available on the San Francisco
Travel website, or at the Visitor
Information Center (900 Market St).
www.sanfrancisco.travel/deals

8 At some Mexican places in the
Mission, delicious burritos and tacos
are under $5. Chinese restaurants and
food trucks also offer good value.

9 Muni has 1-day and 1-month passes
offering great savings. The Clipper Pass
is an all-in-one prepay pass, accepted
on most transport (see pp134–5).

10 The FunCheap website has up-to-
date free and inexpensive activities
and events. Watch the "today" and
"weekend" calendars for what's free.
www.sf.funcheap.com

🔟 Festivals and Parades

1 Chinese New Year
Jan or Feb

This is the biggest Chinese New Year celebration outside Asia. It incorporates traditional displays and the parade of dragons and performers that winds through the streets of Chinatown.

Performer, Chinese New Year parade

2 St. Patrick's Day Parade
Sat or Sun before Mar 17

With San Francisco's large Irish population, not to mention the 25 or so Irish pubs scattered around town, the St. Patrick's Day Parade and the revelry that follows into the night is one of the city's largest celebrations. The parade journeys from 2nd and Market Streets to the Civic Center.

3 Cherry Blossom Festival
Two weekends in Apr

Japantown (see p103) comes to life spectacularly when the cherry trees blossom during April. There are displays of traditional arts and crafts, *taiko* drumming, martial arts demonstrations, and dancing, as well as delicious Japanese food, making this one of the city's favorite celebrations. There is also a colorful and impressive parade.

4 Cinco de Mayo
Sat or Sun before May 5

Commemorating the defeat of the French army at Puebla, Mexico, in 1862, by General Ignacio Zaragoza, this is one of the Latino community's biggest annual festivals, featuring parades, fireworks, music, and dancing. In addition to the Civic Center, much of the fun happens in the Mission District.

5 Carnaval
Mission District ▪ Last weekend in May

Having nothing at all to do with Lent or any other traditional date, San Francisco's Carnaval is staged when the weather will most likely be at its best for the glittery event. Groups work all year long, with the help of municipal grants, to create their dazzling costumes and put together their infectiously rhythmic routines, all to a samba, rumba, or salsa beat.

6 Pride Celebration Parade
Sun in late Jun

More than 300,000 people attend this amazing gay event, the largest of its kind in the US, that takes over Market Street, from the Civic Center to the Embarcadero. It's up to 4 hours of Dykes on Bikes®, drag queens in nuns' habits, gay marching

Pride Celebration

Airshow, Fleet Week

bands, muscle men, and much more. The floats – as well as the cheering throngs – are likely to be the most over-the-top, outlandish things you've ever witnessed.

⑦ Stern Grove Festival
Sun, early Jun–late Aug

A much-loved San Francisco tradition, this festival showcases every kind of music in an idyllic atmosphere (see p118).

⑧ Independence Day
Jul 4

This festival, held from Aquatic Park to PIER 39, involves live entertainment, food stalls, and fireworks launched from several points along the Bayfront. If it's foggy, the bursts of light seem even more romantic.

⑨ Fleet Week
Oct

A celebration of US naval forces, air shows, and a parade of ships sail into the Bay set against the spectacular San Francisco skyline.

⑩ Hallowe'en
Oct 31

This boisterous Castro party and parade is a time for dress-up, dress-down, or undress, as the case may be; let your imagination run wild.

TOP 10 FAIRS AND GATHERINGS

Fillmore Street Jazz Festival

1 Bay to Breakers
Late May
Runners race in funny costumes from the Ferry Building to Ocean Beach.

2 Haight Street Fair
Jun
You'll see hippiedom is still alive after attending this Gathering of the Tribe.

3 North Beach Festival
Jun
The city's oldest street fair features arts and crafts and some great Italian food.

4 Fillmore Street Jazz Festival
Early Jul
Playing up the jazz heritage of this area, with crafts and live music.

5 Folsom Renaissance Faire
Late Aug–early Oct: Sat–Sun
This delightfully rowdy event re-creates Elizabethan England.

6 Ghirardelli Square Chocolate Festival
Early Sep
A chocoholic's dream, with the chance to sample various nibbles.

7 Folsom Street Fair
Last Sun Sep
One of the biggest events for the gay community after Pride.

8 Castro Street Fair
Early Oct
A build-up to Hallowe'en, it focuses attention on everyday gay life.

9 Tet Festival
Jan–Feb
A multicultural party, but mainly Vietnamese-American.

10 Tribal, Folk, & Textile Arts Show
Early Feb
Arts and crafts fair at the Fort Mason Center, with pottery, jewelry, and more.

San Francisco
Area by Area

The Downtown skyline behind the "Painted Ladies" of Alamo Square

10 Downtown

Chinatown statue

The Downtown area is small but highly variegated, including some of the city's oldest and newest landmarks. Colorful Chinatown, exuberant North Beach, posh Nob and Russian Hills, the bustling Financial District, the graceful Ferry Building, and the architecture and culture of Civic Center; all these and more are packed into the city's heart. This is where you can ride the cable cars' most scenic routes *(see pp14–15)* and climb up Telegraph Hill, where Coit Tower stands as one of the city's most loved landmarks, competing with the Transamerica Pyramid not far away.

AREA MAP OF DOWNTOWN

1 **Top 10 Sights**
see pp87–9

1 **Places to Eat**
see p95

1 **Shopping**
see p93

1 **Cafés and Bars**
see p94

1 **North Beach Sights**
see p92

1 Chinatown

Since its beginnings in the 1850s, this densely populated neighborhood has held its own powerful cultural identity despite every threat and cajolery. To walk along its cluttered, clattering streets and alleys is to be transported to another continent and into another way of life – truly a "city" within the city *(see pp22–3)*.

2 North Beach
MAP L4

This lively neighborhood is the original "Little Italy" of the city, and is still noted for its great Italian restaurants and cafés, mostly lined up along and near Columbus Avenue. In the 1950s, it was also a magnet for the Beat writers and poets, notably Jack Kerouac and Allen Ginsberg *(see p44)*, who brought to the area a bohemian style which it still sports today. This is a great place for nightlife, from the tawdry bawdiness of Broadway strip joints to the simple pleasures of listening to a mezzo-soprano while you sip your cappuccino.

3 Nob Hill
MAP N3

With the advent of the cable car, the highest hill in San Francisco was quickly peopled with the elaborate mansions of local magnates – in particular, the "Big Four" who built the Transcontinental Railroad *(see p47)* – and the name has become synonymous with wealth and power. The 1906 earthquake, however, left only one "palace" standing, now the Pacific Union Club, which still proudly dominates the center of the summit. Today, instead of private mansions, Nob Hill is home to the city's fanciest hotels *(see p142)* and apartment buildings, as well as Grace Cathedral.

4 Russian Hill
MAP M2

Another of San Francisco's precipitous heights, one side of which is so steep you'll find no street at all, only steps. The most famous feature of this hill is the charming Lombard Street switchback – "The World's Crookedest Street" – which attests to the hill's notoriously unmanageable inclines. As with Nob Hill, with the cable car's advent, Russian Hill was claimed by the wealthy, and it maintains a lofty position in San Francisco society to this day. It supposedly took its name from the burial place of Russian fur traders, who were among the first Europeans to ply their trade at this port in the early 1800s.

5 Grace Cathedral
MAP N3 ▪ 1100 California St ▪ (415) 749-6300 ▪ Open 7:30am–6pm Mon–Fri, 8am–5pm Sat, 8am–7pm Sun ▪ www.gracecathedral.org

Inspired by French Gothic architecture yet actually constructed of reinforced concrete, these contradictory qualities have given rise to one of the city's best-loved landmarks.

Stained glass at Grace Cathedral

THE MAKING OF A CITY

The Bay lay undiscovered by Europeans until 1769, and for years was little more than a Mission village (below), becoming Mexican in 1821. Gold was found in 1848 and people from all over the world came to try their luck. At the same time, the US took possession of the West Coast. The Transcontinental Railroad helped to establish its financial base.

7 Exploratorium
MAP L6 ▪ Pier 15, Embarcadero ▪ (415) 563-7337 ▪ See website for opening hours ▪ Adm ▪ www.exploratorium.edu

One of the world's first hands-on science museums, the Exploratorium now stands in a spectacular location on Pier 15. There are close to 600 exhibits that are spread among themed indoor galleries and a large outside space. There are also educational programs, a theater, an interactive gift shop, a Bay Observatory, an outdoor plaza, and cafés (see p67).

6 Jackson Square
MAP M5

This neighborhood by the Transamerica Pyramid (see p50) contains some of the city's oldest buildings. In the 19th century it was notorious for its squalor, and was nicknamed the "Barbary Coast," but brothels and drinking establishments have given way to offices and antiques shops. The blocks around Jackson Street and Hotaling Place feature many original facades.

Jackson Square plaque

8 Financial District
MAP M5

Montgomery Street, now the heart of the Financial District, was once lined with small shops where miners came to weigh their gold dust. It marks roughly the old shoreline of shallow Yerba Buena Cove, which was filled in during the Gold Rush to create more land. Today it is lined with banking "temples" of the early 20th century and modern fabrications of glass and steel. At the end of Market Street stands the renovated Ferry Building, which handled 100,000 commuters per day before the city's bridges were constructed, and is now a bustling meeting spot with cafés and artisan food shops. Its tower is inspired by the Moorish belfry of Seville's cathedral in Spain.

Skyscrapers of the Financial District

Art on display in Union Square

9 Union Square
MAP P4

This important square, which gets its name from the pro-Union rallies held here in the early 1860s, has a $25-million upgraded look that includes performance spaces and grassy terraces. It is now the center for high-end shopping (see p79). With the Financial District on one side and the Theater District on the other, it is most picturesque along Powell Street, where the cable cars pass in front of the historic St. Francis Hotel (see p144). Its central column commemorates Admiral Dewey's victory at Manila Bay during the Spanish-American War of 1898.

10 Civic Center
MAP R1

The city's administrative center is an excellent example of grand Beaux Arts taste (see p50). It is perhaps the most elaborate city center complex in the US and it continues to undergo enhancements. Besides the imposing City Hall, with its vast rotunda and formal gardens, it also includes the War Memorial Opera House, the Louise M. Davies Symphony Hall (see p68), the Herbst Theater, the State Building, the New Main Library, and the Old Main Library, re-inaugurated as the Asian Art Museum.

A WALK AROUND NORTH BEACH

> ▶ **MORNING**

Start at the top of North Beach, on **Telegraph Hill** (see p92), admire the famous views, and visit **Coit Tower** (see p50), making sure to take in the murals. Next, walk down to **Filbert Street** (see p92) and go right a couple of blocks until you get to lovely **Washington Square**, where, at **Saints Peter and Paul Catholic Church**, Marilyn Monroe and local baseball great Joe DiMaggio had their wedding pictures taken (see p92). Continue on along Columbus Avenue to the left and pay a visit to **Caffè Roma** (see p94), where you can indulge in a bit of people-watching. Or, across the street, pay homage to the **US Restaurant** (515 Columbus Ave; (415) 397-5200), which serves some of the best pasta in town.

AFTERNOON

After lunch, take a left on Green Street and go over one block to **Upper Grant** (see p92), with its funky shops and bars, a regular hangout since the 1950s. Turn right on to Vallejo Street, where a visit to the famous **Caffè Trieste** (see p94) for a coffee and the authentic bohemian atmosphere is a must. Continue on down Columbus to William Saroyan Place at No. 12 you'll find Specs', an exuberant bar filled with Beat memorabilia. Finally, just across Columbus at No. 261 is the immortal **City Lights Bookstore** (see p92), where you can browse the Beat poetry written by owner Lawrence Ferlinghetti and friends.

See map on p86 ←

North Beach Sights

Coit Tower mural

1 Telegraph Hill
MAP L5

Named after the semaphore installed on its crest in 1850. The hill's eastern side was dynamited to provide rocks for landfill. Steps descend its slopes, lined with gardens. At its summit is Coit Tower.

2 North Beach Views

The panoramic views from both the hill and the top of the Coit Tower are justly celebrated. The wide arc sweeping from the East Bay and the Bay Bridge to Alcatraz and the Golden Gate Bridge is breathtaking.

3 Coit Tower Murals
MAP L5

The frescoes were painted by local artists in 1934, to provide jobs during the Depression *(see p51)*. The murals give sociopolitical commentary yet are also appealing for their details of life in California at the time.

4 Broadway
MAP M5

Made famous in the 1960s for its various adult entertainments. The offerings haven't changed much, though today many venues are now more mainstream.

5 City Lights Bookstore
MAP M4 ▪ 261 Columbus Ave ▪ (415) 362-8193

The Beat poet Lawrence Ferlinghetti founded City Lights in 1953. It's a great place to leaf through a few volumes of poetry or the latest free papers to find out what's on.

6 Filbert Street Steps
MAP L5

The flowery descent down these steps provides great Bay views.

7 Upper Grant
MAP L4

Saloons, cafés, and bluesy music haunts give this northerly section of Grant Avenue a very alternative feel.

8 Caffè Trieste

If you're in the neighborhood on a Saturday afternoon, don't miss the spirited opera that takes place here, one of the longest-running musical shows in the city *(see p94)*.

9 Washington Square
MAP L4

This pretty park is lined with Italian bakeries, restaurants, and bars. Don't be surprised to see practitioners of tai chi doing their thing on the lawn every morning.

10 Saints Peter and Paul Church
MAP L4 ▪ 666 Filbert St ▪ Open daily ▪ Free

Neo-Gothic in conception, with an Italianesque facade, this church is also called the Italian Cathedral and the Fisherman's Church, since many Italians who originally lived in the neighborhood made their living by fishing *(see p48)*.

Saints Peter and Paul Church

Previous pages Aerial view of Alcatraz Island

Shopping

Interior of Schein & Schein

1 Schein & Schein
MAP G2 ■ 1435 Grant Ave ■ (415) 399-8882

Antique maps and prints, fine engravings, rare books, and unique items fill this quaint shop. The owner, Jimmie Schein, is a rich source of local history.

2 W. Graham Arader III
MAP M5 ■ 435 Jackson St, Jackson Square ■ (415) 788-5115 ■ Dis. access

One of the most appealing shops in Jackson Square is like an art museum, featuring fine antique prints. You can marvel at treasures like Audubon's *Birds of America*, ancient maps, and historic prints.

3 Carrots
MAP M5 ■ 843 Montgomery St ■ (415) 834-9040 ■ Dis. access

This beautiful boutique selling women's clothing is located in a charming brick building near Jackson Square.

4 Little Vine
MAP P4 ■ 1541 Grant Ave ■ (415) 738-2221

Grab one of the sandwich specials while browsing this quaint, European-inspired shop, filled with independently produced wines, artisan cheeses, pickles, and locally sourced honey.

5 Serge Sorokko Gallery
MAP P4 ■ 55 Geary St ■ (415) 421-7770

If you're in the market for a piece by one of the modern masters, this is an excellent place to browse important prints and other works by Picasso, Matisse, Mirò, Chagall, and other 20th-century greats, such as Tapiès, Bacon, Twombly, and Warhol.

6 Christopher-Clark Fine Art
MAP P4 ■ 377 Geary St ■ (415) 397-7781 ■ Dis. access

Another gallery for modern European and American masters. A good stock of Bay Area artists, too.

7 Shreve & Co
MAP P4 ■ 200 Post St at Grant ■ (415) 421-2600 ■ Dis. access

A San Francisco original and one of the most elegant jewelers to be found in the city. In addition to gems set in wonderful ways, you'll also find fine timepieces, Limoges porcelain, and Lalique crystal.

8 The North Face
MAP P4 ■ 180 Post St ■ (415) 433-3223 ■ Dis. access

Another San Francisco original. You'll find everything for the outdoor adventurer at this popular chain.

9 Macchiarini Creative Design
MAP G2 ■ 1544 Grant Ave ■ (415) 982-2229

The oldest ongoing arts design house, production studio, and gallery in the US, hand-crafting individually made sculptures and jewelry.

10 William Stout Architectural Books
MAP M4 ■ 804 Montgomery St ■ (415) 391-6757

A landmark for design buffs all over the world, this small shop is divided into two spaces, with newer books on display upstairs.

See map on p86

Cafés and Bars

Brightly painted and welcoming exterior of Caffè Trieste

① Caffè Trieste
MAP M4 ▪ 609 Vallejo St
▪ (415) 982-2605 ▪ Dis. access

One of the most authentic cafés in the city, rich with an arty sense of nonchalance *(see p76)*.

② Tosca
MAP M4 ▪ 242 Columbus Ave
▪ Closed L ▪ (415) 986-9651
▪ Dis. access

Dating back to 1919, this North Beach bar is a celebrity favorite. The jukebox plays opera arias.

③ Caffè Roma
MAP L4 ▪ 526 Columbus Ave
▪ (415) 296-7942 ▪ Dis. access

You're as likely to hear Italian here as you are English. Caffè Roma offers a friendly atmosphere in which to enjoy an espresso and people-watch.

④ Blue Bottle Café
MAP Q4 ▪ 66 Mint St ▪ (510) 653-3394 ▪ Dis. access

A cool, modern space known for its hip crowd, and for turning out some of the city's best coffees *(see p76)*.

⑤ Café de la Presse
MAP N5 ▪ 352 Grant Ave at Sutter ▪ (415) 398-2680

This small corner café carries an impressive assortment of international newspapers, and style and design magazines. Grab a table and just watch the world go by.

⑥ Royal Exchange
MAP N6 ▪ 301 Sacramento St
▪ (415) 956-1710 ▪ Dis. access

For a proper beer and burger, head to this classic watering hole, which has more than 30 beers on tap.

⑦ Le Colonial
MAP N3 ▪ 20 Cosmo Place
▪ (415) 931-3600

Sit back and unwind with a cocktail among the tropical plants at this Vietnamese restaurant. Happy hour is from 5 to 6:30pm daily *(see p71)*.

⑧ Church Key
MAP L4 ▪ 1402 Grant Ave at Green St ▪ (415) 963-1713

This Victorian-themed bar has one of the largest beer selections in San Francisco.

⑨ Bix
MAP M5 ▪ 56 Gold St between Montgomery & Sansome
▪ (415) 433-6300

Tucked into a Downtown alley, this sultry supper club features potent cocktails and smooth jazz.

⑩ Press Club
MAP P4 ▪ 20 Yerba Buena Lane at Market ▪ (415) 744-5000

This popular and ultramodern wine lounge offers a wide selection of wines, as well as a food menu that has been specially crafted to accompany them.

Places to Eat

PRICE CATEGORIES

For a three-course meal for one with half
a bottle of wine (or equivalent meal),
taxes, and extra charges.

$ under $40 $$ $40–$80 $$$ over $80

1 Kokkari Estiatorio
**MAP M6 ■ 200 Jackson St
■ (415) 981-0983 ■ $$**
The Greek cuisine here is a
delectable revelation of flavors.
The lamb shank and grilled
octopus are not to be missed.

2 La Mar
**MAP M6 ■ Pier 1.5
Embarcadero at Washington ■
(415) 397-8880 ■ Closed L ■ $$**
Situated on the waterfront, this
restaurant serves innovative
Peruvian seafood *(see p74)*.

3 One Market
**MAP N6 ■ 1 Market St at
Steuart ■ (415) 777-5577 ■ Closed
Sun ■ Dis. access ■ $$**
The views of the Bay's lights from
here are spectacular at night, and
the farm-fresh food is memorable.

4 Sears Fine Food
**MAP P4 ■ 439 Powell St ■ (415)
986-0700/1160 ■ Dis. access ■ $**
This 1950s retro coffee shop is
famous for its breakfasts, and is
always a reliable choice for a
quick fill-up *(see p77)*.

Sears Fine Food

5 Quince
**MAP M5 ■ 470 Pacific Ave
■ (415) 775-8500 ■ Closed L ■ Dis.
access ■ $$**
The northern Italian cuisine made
with local ingredients has
earned rave reviews for this
Michelin-starred
restaurant *(see p74)*.

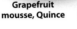

**Grapefruit
mousse, Quince**

6 Slanted Door
**MAP H2 ■ 1 Ferry
Building ■ (415) 861-
8032 ■ Dis. access ■ $$**
This Vietnamese
option, serving
tantalizing dishes,
is a favorite.

7 Gitane
**MAP P4 ■ 6 Claude Lane at
Sutter ■ (415) 788-6686 ■ Closed L
■ Dis. access ■ $$**
Gypsy chic meets classic Iberian
cuisine at this popular restaurant,
which is located on a charming
cobbled alley *(see p74)*.

8 Sotto Mare
**MAP L4 ■ 552 Green St
■ (415) 398-3181 ■ $**
This lively restaurant consistently
turns out terrific Italian seafood
dishes. Be prepared for a wait.

9 Tadich Grill
**MAP N5 ■ 240 California St
■ (415) 391-1849 ■ Dis. access ■ $$**
Beginning life as a coffee stand in
1849, today this traditional
restaurant serves classics such as
clam chowder. Brusque staff add
some fun to the atmosphere. Note
that reservations are not taken.

10 Yank Sing
**MAP H2 ■ 101 Spear St ■ (415)
957-9300 ■ Dis. access ■ $$**
Yank Sing is famous for its signature
Shanghai dumplings, with over
60 varieties on offer. Weekday
lunchtimes can be crowded.

See map on p86 ←

☒☒ The North Shoreline

San Francisco began to grow along the North Shoreline when the Spanish set up a military outpost at the Presidio in 1776. Today the shoreline is a showcase of both historical and modern attractions. The Palace of Fine Arts recalls the 1915 Panama-Pacific International Exposition; the vintage homes of the Marina District have stellar Bay views; ships depart from Pier 41 for Bay cruises; and tourists crowd the stores and seafood eateries of Fisherman's Wharf. Walk all the way from the Golden Gate Bridge to the Embarcadero to get a sense of the many eras of the "Paris of the West."

Embarcadero
street sign

1 Angel and Treasure Islands
Ferries from Pier 41

A trip out to Angel Island, which is now a state park, can make for a very pleasant day of picnicking, biking, hiking, kayaking, and swimming. But in the early 1900s it was the "Ellis Island of the West," where would-be immigrants, mostly Chinese, could be detained for months on end. During World War II, it served as a prisoner of war camp and then later as a missile base. Treasure Island, on the other hand, was built in 1939 for the Golden Gate

International Exposition and served as a US Navy base during World War II. It is now once again owned by the city of San Francisco and has become one of its suburbs.

2 Golden Gate Bridge

This world-famous masterpiece of engineering sets off the entrance to San Francisco Bay in the most spectacular way imaginable, and never fails to elicit gasps of awe from both first-time visitors and old-timers alike. Walking or cycling across its length is an experience not to be missed (see pp12–13).

AREA MAP OF THE NORTH SHORELINE

- **1** Top 10 Sights
  see pp96–9
- ① Places to Eat
  see p101
- ① Wharf Area Shops
  see p100

Alcatraz as seen from the prison gardens

3 Alcatraz

America's "Devil's Island" didn't operate as a prison for a particularly long time, but the cell blocks and control room can still manage to evoke a chill (see pp18–21).

4 Fisherman's Wharf

Although now largely tourist-oriented, there are still authentic maritime sights to see, aromas to savor, and salt air to breathe along these piers (see pp16–17).

5 The Embarcadero
MAP G1

The Embarcadero starts at Aquatic Park and curves all the way around to Hunters Point at the southeastern edge of the city. Since the Port of Oakland handles the shipping needs of the Bay, the old piers are put to use for any number of purposes these days, and the road parallel to them has become a park promenade (see p57). PIER 39 is the most famous among them, since it was turned into an amusement attraction in the 1980s, while other piers house everything from concerts and festivals to antiques fairs and restaurants. When you are looking for a particular pier, note that those to the north of the Ferry Building have odd numbers, while those to the south have even numbers.

View of the Golden Gate Bridge from Crissy Field

6 Crissy Field
MAP D1

Originally marshland and dunes, the field was filled in for the 1915 Panama-Pacific Exposition and paved over for use as an airfield by the army from 1919 to 1936. With the establishment of the Presidio as a national park under the supervision of the city, a massive restoration project has returned part of Crissy Field to wetlands and the rest to lawns, pathways, and picnic areas. The city's 100-acre (40-ha) "Front Yard" is one of the prime viewing sites for the Fourth of July fireworks, while the Golden Gate Promenade is a 3-mile (5-km) paved pathway that runs through this district from Aquatic Park to Fort Point.

7 Fort Point
MAP C1

Crashing waves, passing ships, and windsurfers, along with a Civil War-era fort loaded with cannons, guns, and other military artifacts, make for spectacular photos here beneath the Golden Gate Bridge. You can fish along the seawall and take self-guided or ranger-led tours to learn about the building of the bridge. At the foot of the cliffs on the western side of the fort is a small beach loved by nude sun worshippers (see p12).

8 Aquatic Park
MAP F1 ▪ Visitor Center: 499 Jefferson St ▪ (415) 447-5000 ▪ Open 9:30am–5pm daily

Within the sheltering arm of a curved fishing pier is the warmest, safest Bayside beach. The shallow water is fine for wading and swimming, although it is dependably cold. Joggers and bikers love the paved trail. The cable car turnaround is steps away at Beach and Hyde Streets. In the park you will find a Visitor Center and the Maritime Museum (see p53).

9 The Presidio
MAP D2

This wooded corner of the city has stunning views over the Golden Gate, but from 1776 until 1994 it was occupied by first the Spanish, then

Disney museum exhibit, the Presidio

EARTHQUAKE! THE LANDFILL PROBLEM

Most of the Marina area, as well as the majority of the Financial District, was built on landfill. As time has proven, this was not such a good idea in a seismically active zone. When the Loma Prieta earthquake struck at 5:04pm on October 17, 1989, all such landfills liquefied, gas mains fractured, and several Marina homes slid off their foundations. Buildings that withstand best are those built on bedrock, which includes most of the inland areas of the city.

the Mexican, and finally, the US armies. It is now a major part of the Golden Gate National Recreational Area. It is full of nature trails, streams, forests, drives, and historic structures. Also here is the Walt Disney Family Museum, which gives insight into Walt Disney's life through photographs, animation, and a range of interactive exhibits.

The waterfront by Fort Mason Center

🔟 Fort Mason Center
MAP F1

Since 1976 some of the buildings at this Civil War-era military base have been devoted to cultural programs. Some 50 cultural organizations now call it home. Among the most prominent are the Mexican Museum, the Museo Italo Americano (see p55), the Long Now Foundation, SFMOMA Artists Gallery, the Children's Art Center, the Magic Theatre (see p69), and Herbst Pavilion. The city's finest vegetarian restaurant, Greens, is also here, enjoying views of the Bay (see p74).

A BIKE RIDE THROUGH THE PRESIDIO

▶ Beginning at the Visitor Information Center, where you can pick up an excellent map, first explore the **Main Post**. Here you can ride around the Parade Ground and see the earliest surviving buildings of the Presidio, dating from the 1860s, as well as 18th-century Spanish adobe wall fragments in the former Officers' Club.

Exit the area on Sheridan Avenue, which takes you past the Spanish Colonial Revival-style **Golden Gate Club**, and turn left onto Lincoln Boulevard, which winds its way around the **National Military Cemetery**. Turn right on McDowell Avenue; on the left you will see the Colonial Revival **Cavalry Barracks**.

Now go past the five brick Stables, off to both the left and the right, and stop at the quirky **Pet Cemetery** on the left, where guard dogs are buried as well as many family pets. Next, head under Highway 101 to encounter **Stilwell Hall**, built in 1921 as enlisted barracks and a mess hall for the airmen. Turn left to take in the metal Aerodrome Hangars from the same era, then proceed on and pause at **Crissy Field** to admire the views.

Double back at this point to take the next left down toward the Bay itself and join the Golden Gate Promenade all the way out to **Fort Point**. As long as the fog is not too bad, this is the perfect spot to experience the awe-inspiring **Golden Gate Bridge** (see pp12–13) and the crashing waves of the mighty Pacific.

See map on pp96–7

Fisherman's Wharf Area Shops

1 Ghirardelli Chocolate
MAP K2 ▪ Ghiradelli Square, 900 North Point St ▪ (415) 447-2846

Stop by for a free sample and then stock up on your mouthwatering favorites. If you're feeling nostalgic, take home some chocolate cable cars.

Ghiradelli Chocolate

2 Gigi + Rose
MAP K2 ▪ Ghiradelli Square, 900 North Point St ▪ (415) 765-9060

Whimsical souvenirs fill this lovely shop selling unique accessories, children's outfits, and shoes all designed by the owners.

3 One of a Kind
MAP K2 ▪ Ghiradelli Square, 900 North Point St ▪ (415) 776-3200

This aptly named boutique features beautifully crafted wooden pieces, including jewelry boxes, hand-carved animals, and coffee tables.

4 Lola of North Beach
MAP K2 ▪ Ghiradelli Square, 900 North Point St ▪ (415) 567-7760

Don't miss the wonderful souvenir section, stationery, and locally designed glassware and ornaments at this quaint gift shop.

5 Jackson & Polk
MAP K2 ▪ Ghiradelli Square, 900 North Point St ▪ (415) 345-9708

A little bit of everything is on offer in this boutique of books and treasures, which prides itself on offering a wide selection of San Francisco-based brands.

6 NFL Shop
MAP J4 ▪ PIER 39, Ground Level ▪ (415) 397-2027

This shop is officially licensed to sell products for all major league sports, so this is your chance to stock up on the jerseys, caps, and other merchandise of all your favorite teams.

7 Patagonia
MAP J4 ▪ 700 North Point St ▪ (415) 771-2050

The San Francisco store of this quintessentially Californian company sells classic fleeces and outdoor wear. One percent of annual sales is donated to environmental charities.

8 Cost Plus World Market
MAP K3 ▪ 2552 Taylor St ▪ (415) 928-6200

The original import market that set the trend for all the others. It can still surprise with a well-chosen item from some faraway land.

9 Reader's Bookstore
MAP F1 ▪ Fort Mason Center, Building C ▪ (415) 771-1076

Great secondhand books, records, and CDs, with all the proceeds supporting programs in San Francisco's libraries. You won't find better prices anywhere else.

10 elizabethW
MAP K2 ▪ Ghiradelli Square, 900 North Point St ▪ (415) 441-8354

This boutique offers delightful fragrances, soaps, lotions, sachets, and scented candles, all of which are produced locally.

Local products at elizabethW

Places to Eat

PRICE CATEGORIES
For a three-course meal for one with half
a bottle of wine (or equivalent meal),
taxes, and extra charges.
....
$ under $40 $$ $40–$80 $$$ over $80

1 Gary Danko
MAP K2 ▪ 800 North Point
St at Hyde ▪ (415) 749-2060 ▪ Dis.
access ▪ $$$
The French-American menu allows
you to create your own fixed-price
selection. If you don't have a reserv-
ation (taken two months in advance),
head for the bar, where you can
order anything on the menu.

Interior of Gary Danko restaurant

2 The Codmother
MAP J4 ▪ 2824 Jones St ▪ (415)
606-9349 ▪ Closed D ▪ Dis. access ▪ $
This food truck serves outstanding
fish tacos, fish and chips, and
assorted chip-shop desserts,
such as fried Oreos.

3 Isa
MAP E2 ▪ 3324 Steiner St
between Chestnut & Lombard
▪ (415) 567-9588 ▪ Dis. access ▪ $$
At this tiny Marina restaurant, the
concept is Nouvelle French tapas,
with small plates such as honey-
spiced calamari and lobster broth
sprinkled with tarragon.

4 A16
MAP E1 ▪ 2355 Chestnut St ▪
(415) 771-2216 ▪ Dis. access ▪ $$
An authentic southern Italian dining
experience that's worth getting
dressed up for (see p74).

Exterior of the popular Tacolicious

5 Tacolicious
MAP K4 ▪ 2301 Chestnut St ▪
(415) 346-1966 ▪ $
A multitude of taco choices abound
at this popular joint. Enjoy the free
chips and salsa while you wait.

6 Greens
MAP F1 ▪ Fort Mason Center,
Buchanan St, Building A ▪ (415) 771-
6222 ▪ Dis. access ▪ $$
Since 1979, the inventive vegetarian
dishes plus Bayside panoramas
here add up to a treat (see p74).

7 Zarzuela
MAP L2 ▪ 2000 Hyde St ▪ (415)
346-0800 ▪ Dis. access ▪ $$
Delicious, well-priced tapas is served
up in this cozy restaurant.

8 Scoma's
MAP J2 ▪ Pier 47 on Al Scoma
Way ▪ (415) 771-4383 ▪ Dis. access ▪ $
A Fisherman's Wharf (see p16–17)
seafood tradition since 1965. Enjoy
the cracked crab roasted in garlic.

9 Zushi Puzzle
MAP F2 ▪ 1910 Lombard St ▪
(415) 931-9319 ▪ Closed L ▪ $$
One of the best sushi spots in the
city, thanks to its super-fresh fish
and friendly chef.

10 The Buena Vista Café
MAP K2 ▪ 2765 Hyde St ▪ (415)
474-5044 ▪ Dis. access ▪ $
This café claims to have invented
Irish coffee. The menu features
classic American dishes.

See map on pp96–7

🔟 Central Neighborhoods

Haight Street sign

As is the case with most parts of San Francisco, diversity is the keynote here. This area encompasses the oldest money and the highest society of the founding families of the city, as well as some of its poorest citizens. It takes in the staunchest pillars of the politically savvy. True conservatives are a rarity in this progressive city, but you will find them here alongside the wildest let-it-all-hang-out freethinkers. There's a considerable swath of the comfortably middle-class here too who, like most San Franciscans, are simply intent on enjoying the beauties and pleasures of their great city.

AREA MAP OF CENTRAL NEIGHBORHOODS

1 **Top 10 Sights**
see pp103–5

1 **Places to Eat**
see p107

1 **Shops**
see p106

Grand facades of Pacific Heights

1 Golden Gate Park

One of the largest, finest parks-cum-cultural centers in the world. No visit to the city is complete without taking in some of its wonders (see pp24–5).

2 Union Street
MAP E2

A neighborhood shopping street loaded with tradition, Union Street is noted for its sidewalk cafés, bookstores, and designer boutiques, housed in converted Victorian charmers. The street is at the heart of the Cow Hollow neighborhood, whose name recalls its previous life as a dairy pasture (see p79).

3 Pacific Heights
MAP E2

A grander, more exclusive residential area is hard to imagine. Commanding as it does heights of up to 300 ft (100 m) overlooking the magnificent Bay, every-thing about it proclaims power and wealth. The blocks between Alta Plaza and Lafayette parks are the very heart of the area, but the grandeur extends from Gough to Divisadero Street and beyond. On a sunny day, there's nothing more exhilarat-ing than scaling its hills and taking in the perfectly manicured streets, the to-die-for views, and the palatial dwellings. The Spreckels Mansion, a limestone palace in the Beaux Arts tradition, on Washington and Octavia Streets, is the brightest gem of the lot, now owned by the novelist Danielle Steele.

4 Japantown
MAP F3

This neighborhood has been the focus of the Japanese community since the early 20th century. The Japan Center was built as part of an ambitious 1960s plan to revitalize the Fillmore District. Blocks of aging Victorian buildings were demolished and replaced by the Geary Express-way and this Japanese-style shopping complex with a five-tiered, 75-ft (22-m) Peace Pagoda at its heart. *Taiko* drummers perform here during the Cherry Blossom Festival each April (see p82). The extensive malls are lined with authentic Japanese shops and restaurants, plus an eight-screen cinema, and the Kabuki Springs and Spa. More shops and restaurants can be found along the outdoor mall across Post Street.

Japantown Peace Pagoda

FLOWER POWER

In 1967 San Francisco witnessed the Summer of Love, including a 75,000-strong Human Be-In at Golden Gate Park. People were drawn here – many with flowers in their hair – by the acid-driven melodies of Jefferson Airplane, Janis Joplin, Jimi Hendrix, and The Doors. Love was free, concerts were free, drugs were free, even food and healthcare were free. Soon, however, public alarm, and too many bad trips, caused the bubble to burst.

Geary Boulevard

5 Haight-Ashbury
MAP D4

This anarchic quarter is one of the most scintillating and unconventional in the city, resting firmly on its laurels as ground zero for the worldwide Flower-Power explosion of the 1960s (see p43). Admire the beautiful old Queen Anne-style houses, a few of them still painted in the psychedelic pigments of the hippie era. There are still some tripping freaks and neo-flower children here, along with far-out shops and the venerable Haight-Ashbury Free Clinic. Groove along the street and create your own "Summer of Love." The Lower Haight is noted for its edgy clubs and bars.

6 Geary Boulevard
MAP F3

One of the city's main traffic arteries, sweeping from Van Ness all the way out to Cliff House, Geary Boulevard is a typically unprepossessing urban thoroughfare, but functional. It begins its journey at Market Street, sweeps past Union Square, and then forms the heart of the Theater District, before venturing into the notorious Tenderloin, home to seedy clubs. After it crosses Van Ness, it zips past Japantown and the funky Fillmore District. Soon you're in the Richmond District and before you know it, there's the Pacific Ocean.

7 The Richmond District
MAP C3

This flat district of row houses begins at Masonic Street, sandwiched between Golden Gate Park and California Street. It ultimately extends all the way to the Pacific Ocean, being more and more prone to stay fog-bound the farther west you go. The district is very ethnically diverse and generally middle class. Over the decades, it has been settled by White Russians, East European Jews, and latterly Chinese-Americans and another wave of Russians.

Holy Virgin Cathedral, Richmond District

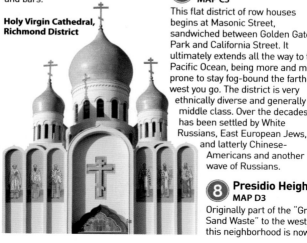

8 Presidio Heights
MAP D3

Originally part of the "Great Sand Waste" to the west, this neighborhood is now one of the most elite of all. The zone centers on Sacramento Street as its discreet shopping area. It's worth a stroll, primarily for the architecture. Of interest are the Swedenborgian Church at 2107 Lyon Street, the Roos House at 3500 Jackson Street, and Temple Emanu-El at 2 Lake Street.

9 Hayes Valley
MAP F4

Rising like a phoenix from the ashes of racial unrest in what used to be a rundown African-American slum, this small area has now become one of San Francisco's hipper shopping and dining districts. The dismantling of an ugly freeway overpass following the 1989 earthquake helped turn the tide, and the welcome result is a chic area that hasn't lost its edge. Hayes Valley festivals take place in midsummer, when the area's streets are thronged with revelers.

Alamo Square, Western Addition

10 Western Addition
MAP E3

This area, too, was once sandy waste, but after World War II the district became populated by Southern African-Americans who came west for work. For a short time, it was famous for jazz and blues clubs, as embodied, until his death in 2001, by John Lee Hooker and his Boom Boom Room. Today, it is still largely African-American in character and rather rundown, although it does include architecturally odd Cathedral of St. Mary of the Assumption (see p48) and photogenic Alamo Square (see p51).

A HIPPIE TOUR OF HAIGHT-ASHBURY

▶ MORNING

Begin at **Alamo Square** (see p51), with the Westerfield House at 1998 Fulton at Scott, former residence of Ken Kesey, the writer and visionary who arguably got the whole 1960s movement going. Walk up Scott, turn right on Page and go to No. 1090, where the rock band Big Brother and the Holding Company got their start. A block and a half farther on, go right on Lyon to No. 112, where Janis Joplin lived for most of 1967 (see p45).

Continue on to the Panhandle, an extension of Golden Gate Park, where in June 1967 the Jimi Hendrix Experience gave a free concert. Now turn left on Central and head up to steep **Buena Vista Park**, site of public Love-Ins in the 1960s and 1970s. Turn right on Haight and check out Positively Haight Street, 1400 Haight Street at Masonic, one of the fanciest hippie shops.

Continue on to the Haight-Ashbury intersection and walk along Haight to Clayton; at No. 558 is the much-loved Haight-Ashbury Free Clinic, still imbued with the spirit of the 1960s. If you are hungry, stop in for a snack at **Blue Front Café** (see p107).

Refreshed, walk towards the park, then turn right on Stanyan all the way to Fulton. At 2400 Fulton stands the former Jefferson Airplane Mansion, which used to be painted black. Finally, head back to **Golden Gate Park** (see pp24–5) and make your way to the drum circles on Hippie Hill to groove to the tribal beats.

See map on p102 ←

Shops

Clothes on sale at Marmalade

1 Marmalade
MAP F2 ■ 1843 Union St ■ (415) 400-4027

A chic yet casual boutique with dresses, tops, and jewelry that are stylish but not overpriced. Marmalade also sells fabulous bags, trinkets, and other great gift items.

2 Enchanted Crystal
MAP F2 ■ 1895 Union St ■ (415) 885-1335

This gallery/store offers an amazing collection of art, glass, handcrafted jewelry, and decorative gifts.

3 Carol Doda's Champagne and Lace Lingerie Boutique
MAP F2 ■ 1850 Union St ■ (415) 776-6900

Bodywear for women and men, brought to you by the infamous entertainment pioneer who gave San Francisco topless dancing in the 1960s. Naturally, the emphasis here is on risqué styles.

4 Brooks Shoes For Kids
MAP E3 ■ 3307 Sacramento St ■ (415) 440-7599

This store specializes in high fashion, with a huge range in all styles on offer. Accessories and toys are also sold here.

5 Past Perfect
MAP D4 ■ 854 Stanyan St ■ (415) 929-2288

There are fair prices and tons to choose from at this huge vintage store. Plan to spend a while perusing their unique furniture, lighting, and art – there is something for everyone here. The staff are friendly, too.

6 Polanco
MAP F4 ■ 393 Hayes St ■ (415) 252-5753

A sophisticated gallery of Mexican arts, which features silver jewelry, colorful Day of the Dead masks and crafts, as well as the work of emerging Mexican artists.

7 Sue Fisher King
MAP F2 ■ 3067 Sacramento St ■ (888) 811-7276

Nearly 40 years ago, Sue Fisher King opened her shop of trinkets and treasures for the home, fine jewelry, and divinely scented bath products. Today it's still considered one of the city's must-visits.

8 Comix Experience
MAP E4 ■ 305 Divisadero St ■ (415) 863-9258

The comics here have adult aficionados in mind: *The Ring of the Nibelung, The Filth, Naughty Bits*, and *Static-X* are just a few examples of the wacky titles that await you in both new and vintage issues.

9 Chronicle Books
MAP F4 ■ 1846 Union St ■ (415) 345-8435

More of a gift shop than a true bookstore, Chronicle Books is also a publisher and stocks its own titles. The store offers a large number of unconventional books, as well as gorgeous cookbooks, and a wide selection of gifts.

10 Amoeba Music
MAP D4 ■ 1855 Haight St ■ (415) 831-1200

Besides thousands of LPs, tapes, and CDs, there's also a huge selection of DVDs and posters at this record store, which is part of an independent chain.

Places to Eat

PRICE CATEGORIES
For a three-course meal for one with half a bottle of wine (or equivalent meal), taxes, and extra charges.

$ under $40 $$ $40–$80 $$$ over $80

German chocolate cake at Absinthe

1 Perry's
MAP F2 ▪ 1944 Union St ▪ (415) 922-9022 ▪ Dis. access ▪ $
A San Francisco institution, noted for its burgers and other all-American favorites, including meatloaf, prime rib, and fried chicken.

2 State Bird Provisions
MAP F3 ▪ 1529 Fillmore St ▪ (415) 795-1272 ▪ $$$
A trendy Michelin-starred restaurant serving small plates of French and American food. Choose most of your food from a cart or tray of dishes brought out by the waiting staff.

3 SPQR
MAP E3 ▪ 1911 Fillmore St ▪ (415) 771-7779 ▪ Dis. access ▪ $$
Reservations are accepted online only at this no-frills, rustic Roman-inspired eatery with mouthwatering antipasti and superior service.

4 Nopa
MAP E4 ▪ 560 Divisadero St ▪ (415) 864-8643 ▪ Closed L ▪ $
Considered one of the best restaurants in the city, Nopa has a seasonally changing menu.

5 Absinthe
MAP F4 ▪ 398 Hayes St ▪ (415) 551-1590 ▪ Dis. access ▪ $$
This Parisian-style bistro serves specials such as confit of Muscovy duck leg with prunes.

6 Pizzeria Delfina
MAP F5 ▪ 2406 California St ▪ (415) 440-1189 ▪ Dis. access ▪ $
Rustic, simple, and fresh, this popular pizzeria serves incredible Neapolitan thin-crust pizzas in addition to delicious, authentic antipasti and salami.

7 Suppenkuche
MAP F4 ▪ 525 Laguna St ▪ (415) 252-9289 ▪ Dis. access ▪ $
With a fun, lively atmosphere, this is an ideal place for enthusiasts of hearty, meaty German food and beer.

8 Kiss Seafood
MAP F3 ▪ 1700 Laguna St ▪ (415) 474-2866 ▪ Dis. access ▪ $$
Book ahead to eat delectable sushi and sashimi at this tiny restaurant.

9 Blue Front Café
MAP E4 ▪ 1430 Haight St ▪ (415) 252-5917 ▪ Dis. access ▪ $
For cheap, tasty Mediterranean wraps and sandwiches, this café is a local favorite.

10 The Grove
MAP E3 ▪ 2016 Fillmore St ▪ (415) 474-1419 ▪ Dis. access ▪ $
It almost feels like a mountain lodge, with lounging furniture and a roaring fire. The tempting menu offers tasty entrées such as chicken pot pie or three-cheese macaroni.

Interior of Nopa

See map on p102

TOP 10 Southern Neighborhoods

The southern part of San Francisco comprises some of the liveliest, most authentic parts of the city – the clubs of SoMa, the gay world of the Castro, and the Latino Mission District. There are also some up-and-coming neighborhoods on this side of the city, such as Bernal Heights and Glen Park, as the more central areas have priced creative types out toward the southern borders. Laid-back Noe Valley was the first such choice for high-rent refugees, but it, too, has become gentrified and pushed people farther south.

Mission Dolores facade detail

AREA MAP OF SOUTHERN NEIGHBORHOODS

1. **Top 10 Sights**
   see pp109–11
1. **Places to Eat**
   see p115
1. **Shops**
   see p112
1. **Bars**
   see p114
1. **Nightclubs**
   see p113

0 meters 800
0 yards 800

1 China Basin
MAP H4

This old shipping port has not been exempt from the upsurge of interest in previously neglected areas. The main change has been wrought by the building of the AT&T Park, home to the San Francisco Giants, the city's major league baseball team, and developers have already put forth ideas for putting the zone to use. A number of restaurants, bars, and clubs, many with port views, have opened up here or have been refurbished.

China Basin statue

2 Mission Dolores

The Spanish Misión San Francisco de Asís, from which the city takes its name, is a marvel of preservation and atmospheric charm. It was founded in 1776, just a few weeks before the Declaration of Independence *(see pp34–5)*.

3 South of Market
MAP R4

The city's erstwhile rough-and-tumble warehouse district has been on the rise for decades and continues to attract arty types as well as a whole range of clubs and cool cafés *(see p33)*.

4 Castro District
MAP E5

This neighborhood, with the landmark Castro Theatre, is the center of San Francisco's gay community. The intersection of Castro and 18th Streets is the self-proclaimed "Gayest Four Corners of the World." This openly homosexual nexus emerged in the 1970s as the place of pilgrimage for gays and lesbians from all over the world. Every Hallowe'en, Castro Street hosts the gay costume party and parade that is one of the city's best, second only to the Gay Pride Parade *(see p83)*.

Castro Theatre

A GAY CITY

After the free-love movement of the 1960s (see p104), homosexuals realized that they, too, had rights to stand up for, and started moving into the Castro in the 1970s. In no time the neighborhood was a nonstop – and unstoppable – party of freewheeling sexual excess. Suddenly gays were "out" in legions, which brought with it political clout. San Francisco is still one of the easiest places in the world to live out an openly gay identity.

5 Yerba Buena Center

This is fast becoming one of San Francisco's leading centers for the performing arts and has a growing number of museums representing the city's ethnic diversity. Every year sees some new addition to the complex (see pp32–3).

6 Twin Peaks
MAP E6

These two hills were first known in Spanish as *El Pecho de la Chola*, or "The Bosom of the Indian Girl." At the top, there is an area of parkland from which you can enjoy incomparable views of the city. There is plenty of parking near the viewing point. If you're up to the climb, take the footpath to the top, above the main viewing area, to get a 360-degree panorama.

Carnaval parade, Mission District

7 Noe Valley
MAP E6

Once a simple working-class neighborhood, until the 1970s brought hippies, gays, artists, and other bohemian types to its slopes and it became an attractive alternative to more established quarters. In its heyday it was known as both "Nowhere Valley" for its relative remoteness, and as "Granola Valley" for its nature-loving denizens. Lately, it has been taken over by middle-class professionals, who value it for its orderliness, but 24th Street still hums with activity and is lined with cafés and bookstores.

8 San Francisco Museum of Modern Art

San Francisco's home for its extensive modern art collection is as impressive outside as it is awe-inspiring inside. Its new extension will enable even more of its stunning treasure of painting, photography, media and digital installations, design, and large-scale sculptures to be on show (see pp30–31).

View of the city from Twin Peaks

A WALK AROUND THE CASTRO DISTRICT

Church Street
Muni Station

Harvey Milk
Plaza

The Cafe

Twin Peaks

Castro Theater

Badlands

Moby Dick

Brand X
Antiques

⑨ Mission District
MAP F5

The Mission is home to many of San Francisco's Latinos. They have brought their culture with them – *taquerías*, salsa clubs, Santería shops, murals, and Spanish everywhere. Its festivals are not to be missed, especially Carnaval *(see p82)*.

⑩ Potrero Hill
MAP H5 ■ Anchor Brewing Co, 1705 Mariposa St ■ (415) 863-8350 ■ www.anchorbrewing.com

This SoMa hill was once set to become the next big thing, but its isolation kept that from happening, cut off from the rest of the city, as it is, by freeways on three sides and its own precipitous inclines. So, it has remained a quiet neighborhood with spectacular views. To be sure, a few upmarket concerns are located here, and there are restaurants, bars, and many design stores, but mostly it is residential. One tourist sight of note is the Anchor Brewing Company. It's worth a visit, especially as the walking tour and tasting session are free. There are only two tours each weekday; you must phone to book.

▶ Begin at the gay mecca of San Francisco, the **Church Street Muni Station** on Upper Market. Decades ago, this corner developed a gay identity as the beginning point of the Castro neighborhood, but it is on the next block, between Sanchez and Noe, that the gay shops and venues really begin to proliferate. Towards the corner of Castro is **The Cafe** at 2369 Market, offering a range of strong drinks accompanied by Top 40 mixes.

Continuing on to Castro Street, take in **Harvey Milk Plaza**, with its huge rainbow flag; the plaza is named after the slain gay leader *(see p47)*. On the opposite corner, check out **Twin Peaks** *(see p73)* at 401 Castro, the oldest totally "out" gay bar, notable for its picture windows affording a full view of goings-on, both inside and on the street outside.

Pushing on to No. 429, allow the **Castro Theatre** to capture your attention. One of the city's most ornate cinema palaces, it hosts innumerable premieres of gay-themed films. Farther along at No. 570, **Brand X Antiques** *(see p112)* is a great place to browse, with its eclectic collection of goods, ranging from furniture to homoerotica. One block over, on Hartford Street, **Moby Dick** *(see p72)* is a popular spot that attracts a steady crowd of regulars. Stop here to shoot some pool or pinball while enjoying 1980s tunes.

Finally, just up 18th Street at No. 4121 is **Badlands** *(see p73)*, a cruisy pickup scene that packs them in, especially after 10pm.

See map on pp108–9

Shops

① Needles & Pens
MAP F4 ■ 3253 16th St ■
(415) 255-1534

There's a little bit of everything at this funky, eclectic store. Don't miss the fantastic magazine selection, unique cards, stationery, and T-shirts, as well as the gallery.

② Jeremy's
MAP R6 ■ 2 South Park ■
(415) 882-4929

A fabulous discount boutique for men's and women's fashions, including Prada, Gucci, Armani, Ralph Lauren, DKNY, Dior, and Anthropologie – all at reduced prices.

③ Borderlands Books
MAP F5 ■ 866 Valencia St ■
(415) 824-8203

A funky bookstore specializing in science fiction, horror, and fantasy. Whether these genres are your cup of tea or not, Borderlands is worth a visit for a dose of the unusual.

④ Brand X Antiques
MAP E5 ■ 570 Castro St ■
(415) 626-8908

The gay couple who own this shop share a discerning and humorous eye for antiques. In addition to baubles, rings, and furniture, the collection also features tongue-in-cheek vintage homoerotica.

⑤ The Voyager Shop
MAP F5 ■ 365 Valencia St ■
(415) 779-2712

A unique retail store of worldwide treasures, with everything from clothing and accessories to stationery and ocean gear – and a full gallery to boot.

⑥ Paxton Gate
MAP F5 ■ 824 Valencia St ■
(415) 824-1872

This wonderland of unique items for gifts and home decor even includes strange pieces of taxidermy. Kids will love this place as much as adults do.

⑦ Astrid's Rabat Shoes
MAP F6 ■ 3909 24th St ■
(415) 282-7400

If walking the steep city streets is challenging your footwear, this Noe Valley store can fit you with a new pair of sturdy, not to mention stylish, walking shoes.

⑧ City Art Gallery
MAP F5 ■ 828 Valencia St ■
(415) 970-9900

This gallery sells work from dozens of local artists in a variety of media. Much of it is reasonably priced, making it a great spot to find a unique gift.

⑨ Botanica Yoruba
MAP F5 ■ 3423 19th St ■
(415) 814-3130

The Santería religion is the faith of many Latinos, and this shop fulfills their ritualistic and spiritual needs. An array of potions and powders, candles, and icons (see p49).

⑩ Fatto a Mano
MAP G4 ■ 129 Carolina St ■
(415) 525-4348

Owned by a husband-and-wife team, this store sells unique home furnishings, including ceramics, glassware, and kitchen accessories. Their beautiful handmade furnishings are imported from Italy.

Treasures and taxidermy, Paxton Gate

Nightclubs

1 The Stud Bar
MAP G4 ▪ 399 9th St at Harrison ▪ (415) 863-6623

Around for over 35 years, this formerly exclusive enclave of maleness is now popular with anybody who enjoys a rollicking lusty time. Theme nights include Trannyshack, which is a fabulous drag cabaret show.

2 Make-Out Room
MAP F5 ▪ 3225 22nd St at Mission ▪ (415) 647-2888

Cool live music and DJ nights make this a Mission favorite. The decor is original, the drinks are cheap (particularly during the nightly happy hour), and the staff is appropriately witty.

3 The Café
MAP E5 ▪ 2369 Market St at Castro ▪ (415) 861-3846

There is something (and somebody) for everybody at this camp, cruisy Castro old-timer that attracts gays, lesbians, and straights in equal doses. The outdoor balcony is great for people-watching.

4 AsiaSF
MAP G4 ▪ 201 9th St at Howard ▪ (415) 255-2742

Brazen Asian drag queens are your waitresses, who also perform bartop and stage numbers. The tropical cocktails glow in the dark. There are DJs and dancing downstairs.

5 The EndUp
MAP R4 ▪ 401 6th St at Harrison ▪ (415) 357-0827

Formerly exclusively gay, as famously featured in *Tales of the City* by Armistead Maupin *(see p45)*, this classic is now thoroughly mixed, featuring house music and an all-day Sunday "T" Dance.

6 Café du Nord
MAP F4 ▪ 2170 Market St ▪ (415) 861-5016

Located in the landmark Swedish-American building, this subterranean

Entrance to Café du Nord nightclub

nightclub is one of the smartest the city has to offer. It also hosts local and national bands.

7 111 Minna Gallery
MAP P5 ▪ 111 Minna St between New Montgomery & 2nd ▪ (415) 974-1719

Part gallery, part lounge, Minna is a fun place to grab a drink Downtown, and there's almost always some event happening here.

8 El Rio
MAP F5 ▪ 3158 Mission St ▪ (415) 282-3325

Different dance events every night of the week draw a diverse crowd ready to work their thing at this bar on the go since 1978 – Sunday Salsa Showcase is particularly popular.

9 Elbo Room
MAP F5 ▪ 647 Valencia St ▪ (415) 552-7788

This two-story bar combines dancing, live entertainment, and pool tables. A great mix of people come together here for the welcoming atmosphere and a great time.

10 Mighty
MAP G4 ▪ 119 Utah St at 15th ▪ (415) 762-0151

Popular hip-hop and house DJs keep the crowds dancing at this large nightclub, which also doubles as an art gallery *(see p70)*.

See map on pp108–9

Bars

1 Lucky 13
MAP F4 ▪ 2140 Market St at Church ▪ (415) 487-1313

This no-frills, punk-rock dive bar has a chilled-out vibe. The jukebox is full of indie alternative sounds and there is free popcorn.

2 Bottom of the Hill
MAP G4 ▪ 1233 17th St between Texas & Missouri ▪ (415) 626-4455

This legendary live-music venue features an assortment of punk, rock, and folk bands, plus a pleasant back patio for beer breaks (see p70).

3 Nihon Whisky Lounge
MAP F4 ▪ 1779 Folsom at 14th St ▪ (415) 552-4400

The white-pebbled floor and vast selection of hard-to-find whiskeys make this Japanese whiskey lounge a super-cool spot to grab a drink.

Rare whiskey, Nihon Whisky Lounge

4 Twenty Five Lusk
MAP H3 ▪ 25 Lusk St ▪ (415) 495-5875

Located in a renovated timber warehouse, this elegant bar-cum-restaurant is sleek and modern with a hip, urban vibe. The cocktails are delicious and the stylish lounge below is great for people-watching.

5 The Residence
MAP F4 ▪ 718 14th St ▪ (415) 797-8866

Friendly bartenders keep people coming to this neighborhood hang-out with comfy chairs and a cozy, relaxed interior. There is a good selection of beer and cocktails.

6 Trick Dog
MAP F5 ▪ 3010 20th St ▪ (415) 471-2999

Well-crafted and imaginative cocktails win rave reviews at this

The bar at Trick Dog

beautiful, split-level bar in the Mission District. Innovative decor and delicious bar snacks.

7 The Knockout
MAP F6 ▪ 3223 Mission St ▪ (415) 550-6994

With DJs and live music all week, and bingo on Thursdays, The Knockout has remained one of the most popular dive bars in San Francisco for years.

8 Mezzanine
MAP Q3 ▪ 444 Jesse St ▪ (415) 625-8880

This richly diverse gathering space showcases live and electronic music from a wide variety of genres (including rock, dance, hip-hop, soul, jazz, salsa, and world beat), as well as hosting multimedia art events and fashion shows (see p70).

9 83 Proof
MAP P6 ▪ 83 1st St ▪ (415) 296-8383

This popular neighborhood hangout is often crowded with locals, who come here for the inventive drinks made from the five shelves of liquor behind the bar.

10 21st Amendment
MAP R6 ▪ 563 2nd St ▪ (415) 369-0900

A sports fan's dream, this brewpub near the ballpark serves up handcrafted beers and standard American fare. It's a friendly place to catch a game on television.

Places to Eat

PRICE CATEGORIES
For a three-course meal for one with half a bottle of wine (or equivalent meal), taxes, and extra charges.

$ under $40 $$ $40–$80 $$$ over $80

1 Stable Café
MAP F5 ▪ 2128 Folsom at 17th St ▪ (415) 552-1199 ▪ Closed D ▪ $
Stable Café serves delicious home-made breakfast and lunch options that center heavily on fresh-baked breads and healthy local ingredients.

2 Marlowe
MAP H3 ▪ 500 Brannan St ▪ (415) 974-5599 ▪ Dis. access ▪ $$
This cozy yet chic restaurant serves outstanding bistro dishes.

3 Prospect
MAP H2 ▪ 300 Spear St ▪ (415) 247-7770 ▪ $$$
One of the city's seminal dinners out can be had at this SoMa mainstay. The decadent brunch is less pricey.

4 Sparky's Pizza & Diner
MAP F4 ▪ 242 Church St at Market ▪ (415) 626-8666 ▪ $
Open 24 hours, this café is great for clubbers wanting to grab a late-night breakfast or burger and fries.

5 Chow
MAP F4 ▪ 215 Church St ▪ (415) 552-2469 ▪ Dis. access ▪ $
Just off Market Street, Chow offers affordable pizzas, pastas, and grilled

and roasted meats, as well as a selection of beers and wines. The service is friendly.

6 Pancho Villa Taqueria
MAP F4 ▪ 3071 16th St ▪ (415) 864-8840 ▪ Dis. access ▪ $
This is one of the best Mexican eateries in the city, serving up authentic tacos and burritos for ridiculously low prices.

7 Range
MAP F5 ▪ 842 Valencia St ▪ (415) 282-8283 ▪ Dis. access ▪ $$
This sleek Mission District restaurant serves simple classics and is a perfect end to a day's sightseeing.

8 Caffè Centro
MAP R6 ▪ 102 South Park ▪ (415) 882-1500 ▪ Closed Sun ▪ Dis. access ▪ $
A brisk business in drinks, pastries, soups, and salads. Always crowded.

9 Osha Thai
MAP F5 ▪ 819 Valencia St ▪ (415) 826-7738 ▪ Dis. access ▪ $
A perennial favorite with the club crowd. Dishes are fresh and tasty, service is lightning fast, and prices are extremely reasonable.

10 Delfina
MAP F5 ▪ 3261 18th St ▪ (415) 552-4055 ▪ Closed L ▪ Dis. access ▪ $$
Delfina serves perfect Italian fare. Its next-door pizzeria is ideal for a more casual dinner (see p75).

Interior of Italian restaurant Delfina

See map on pp108–9

🔟 Oceanfront

As with every part of the city, this area is a study in contrasts. It contains terrains of natural, untamed beauty – particularly the windswept cliffs and hidden ravines of Land's End, the scene of innumerable shipwrecks. Yet, just a few blocks away is Sea Cliff, one of the most exclusive residential neighborhoods. Of all the city's areas, this is where you're almost certain to encounter the infamous fog, but if the weather is clear there are great views of the offshore Seal Rocks and even the Farallon Islands.

Statue at Legion of Honor

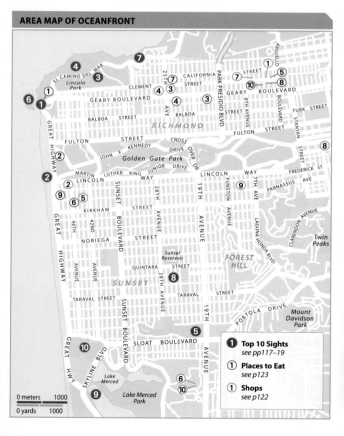

AREA MAP OF OCEANFRONT

❶ **Top 10 Sights**
see pp117–19

① **Places to Eat**
see p123

① **Shops**
see p122

0 meters 1000
0 yards 1000

1 Cliff House
MAP A3 ▪ (415) 386-3330 ▪
Open for lunch and dinner (call for
times) ▪ www.cliffhouse.com

Built in 1909, the present structure is
the third on this site and was
renovated in 2004. Its predecessor, a
massively elaborate eight-story
Victorian-Gothic castle that burned
down in 1907, was built by the
flamboyant entrepreneur Adolph
Sutro (his estate overlooking Cliff
House is now Sutro Heights Park).
Cliff House has restaurants on the
upper levels, observation decks
overlooking the Pacific Ocean, a wing
containing two bars, and the Camera
Obscura, which gives a close-up view
of Seal Rocks (see p118).

2 Ocean Beach
MAP A4 ▪ The Great Hwy

Most of the western boundary of San
Francisco is defined by this broad
sweep of sand. Although it is a
sublime sight when viewed from Cliff
House or Sutro Heights Park, do
note that the beach is dangerous
to swim from due to its icy waters,
rough shore breakers, and, most
of all, rip currents that are powerful
enough to drag even strong
swimmers out to sea. Nevertheless,
hardy Californian surfers in thick
wetsuits are a common sight here,
and in fine weather sunbathers and
picnickers materialize to loll on the
sand and enjoy the sunshine.

3 Legion of Honor
MAP B3 ▪ Lincoln Park, 34th
Ave & Clement St ▪ (415) 750-3600
Open 9:30am–5:15pm Tue–Sun ▪
Adm ▪ www.fams.org

The creation of Alma de Bretteville
Spreckels, heiress to the Spreckels
sugar fortune, this museum is a
replica of the Palais de la Légion
d'Honneur in Paris. The original
structure was built for the 1915
Panama-Pacific Exposition, but Mrs.
Spreckels wanted to build a permanent version and employed the same
architect she commissioned for her
mansion in Pacific Heights (see
p103). It opened in 1924 and features
medieval to 20th-century European
art, with paintings by Monet and
Rembrandt. The museum also hosts
excellent traveling exhibitions.

4 Oceanfront Parks
MAP A3

Lincoln Park, Lands End, and Sutro
Heights Park are large green areas
overlooking the coast all along this
northwestern corner of the peninsula. Lincoln Park is the work of
John McClaren (see p25), and
features trails with some of the best
views of the Golden Gate Bridge.
Lands End is a rugged stretch along
the cliffs that features a picturesque
cove and truly spectacular hiking.
Statuary of the old Sutro estate still
decorates Sutro Heights Park, which
dominates the coastal scene from its
dramatic vantage point.

Rock labyrinth by Eduardo Aguilera at Lands End

⑤ Sigmund Stern Grove
Sloat Blvd at 19th Ave, Sunset ■
(415) 252-6252 ■ **www.sterngrove.org**
This 63-acre (25-ha) ravine in the
southern Sunset District was
donated to the city of San Francisco
by Rosalie M. Stern in 1931, in
memory of her husband Sigmund,
a civic leader. It is the site of the
nation's original free summer arts
festival, Stern Grove Festival, which
was endowed in 1938 and is still in
operation today. Running on Sunday
afternoons, the program may include
classical music performed by the
San Francisco Symphony Orchestra,
opera, jazz, popular music, or
productions by the San Francisco
Ballet. The natural amphitheater, in a
eucalyptus, fir, and redwood grove,
has great acoustics.

⑥ Seal Rocks
MAP A3
The westernmost promontory on
this tip of the peninsula is Point
Lobos, the projection that forms
the rocky cove of Land's End.
Along to the south from here down
to Cliff House is a scattering of
small, rocky islands that are
frequented by seals – hence the
name. Bring binoculars with you to
spy on the seals and birds in their
natural habitat. At night, from the
beach or Cliff House promenade, the
barking of the sea lions – like the
keening of the foghorns – is both
reassuring and eerie, and so very
"San Francisco." On a clear day, 32
miles (50 km) off the coast, you can
see the Farallon Islands, which are
also inhabited by sea lions and have
a state-protected rookery.

Seals basking on the Seal Rocks

CLIFF HOUSE AND THE SUTRO BATHS
Adolph Sutro came to San Francisco
from Prussia in 1851, aged 21 and
looking for gold. He became "King of
the Comstock Lode" in Nevada, and
brought his riches back to the city to
invest them in land. His projects included building the first Cliff House, the
popular Sutro Baths, and his own lavish
estate. In the process, he made the
Ocean Beach area into a recreational
gem. The legacy lives on, despite the
disappearance of all three of the
famous buildings he constructed.

⑦ Sea Cliff
MAP C2
Many famous actors, such as Robin
Williams and Sharon Stone, have had
homes in this elite residential
enclave, which stands in stark
contrast to the natural coastal area
all around it. Most of the luxurious
homes are Mediterranean in style
and date from the 1920s. Just below
the neighborhood, China Beach –
named after poor Chinese fishermen
who used to camp here – is one of
the safest beaches in the city for
swimming and is equipped with
showers and other facilities. Baker
Beach, just to the north, is another
popular beach *(see pp58–9)*.

⑧ Sunset District
MAP C5 ■ **Between Sloat Blvd
& Golden Gate Park and Stanyan St &
the Pacific Ocean**
Like its counterpart, the Richmond
District *(see p104)*, this neighborhood
was part of the Outer Lands and is
purely residential, consisting of row

upon row of neat, look-alike houses. Yet, like the entire area along the ocean, this district is subject to a great deal of gray weather. Its one claim to fame is Sutro Tower, the pronged red-and-white television antenna that resembles something out of a science fiction movie.

9 Lake Merced
Hwy 35

Located at the beginning of scenic Skyline Boulevard (Hwy 35), this attractive lake, set amid verdant hills, extends across the southern end of the Sunset District. Relatively undeveloped and certainly under-used, it nevertheless gets its share of recreation enthusiasts. They come for the municipal 18-hole Harding Park Golf Course, as well as the biking and running trails that circle the lake's green shoreline.

Fishing boats on Lake Merced

10 San Francisco Zoo
Sloat Blvd at Pacific Ocean ▪ Buses 18 & 23 ▪ (415) 753-7080 ▪ Open 10am–5pm daily ▪ Dis. access ▪ Adm ▪ www.sfzoo.org

San Francisco Zoo is at the far southwest corner of the city, between the Pacific Ocean and Lake Merced. The complex is home to more than 1,000 species. Gorilla Preserve, Grizzly Gulch, Koala Crossing, and Children's Zoo are particular hits, as are the feeding times for the grizzly bears and the penguins. Summer brings a busy program of extra activities in the Children's Zoo.

A TWO-HOUR HIKE AROUND LAND'S END

This section of the coast is amazingly wild, especially considering that it is actually within the city limits. Note that portions of the hike are very rugged, so dress accordingly, with good footwear.

Begin at the far end of the **Merrie Way** parking lot and take the steps down. Follow the trail that passes by the **Sutro Baths** ruins, to your left as you descend. Continue on along to the Overlook, from which you can take in **Seal Rocks** and much of the Pacific panorama.

Now double back a bit to pick up the trail that continues along the coast. You will see the remains of concrete military bunkers, which have been broken and tilted by the unstable land, and are now decorated with graffiti. Soon you come to a beach below rocky cliffs; note that the surging water is very unpredictable here, so be very attentive. Continue walking and you will arrive at **Land's End Cove**, where a makeshift beach, using rock walls as windbreakers, is popular with nudists.

Next, climb up one of the sets of wooden steps to join the path up above and continue on around the bend, where a stunning view of the **Golden Gate Bridge** (see pp12–13) will greet you. Continue walking all the way to **Eagle's Point** and then return by way of the higher trail that winds through **Lincoln Park** (see p117).

If you have worked up an appetite from your hike, enjoy a meal and the wonderful views at **Cliff House** (see p123).

See map on p116 ←

Shops

1 Park Life
MAP D3 ■ 220 Clement St ■ (415) 386-7275

Part retail store, part art gallery, this sleek space features limited-edition books, prints, homeware, jewelry, T-shirts, and art. The gallery exhibits contemporary art.

2 The Last Straw
MAP A5 ■ 4540 Irving St ■ (415) 566-4692

This tiny store on the beach has been run by the same friendly owner for more than 30 years. Great, interesting pieces of jewelry and unique finds are on sale here.

3 Gaslight and Shadows Antiques
MAP C3 ■ 2335 Clement St ■ (415) 387-0633

The specialty here is porcelain, specifically the delicate master-pieces turned out by the various makers in the town of Limoges, France. It's like visiting a museum dedicated to this fine art form. There are dolls and costume jewelry, too.

4 Paul's Hat Works
MAP B3 ■ 6128 Geary Blvd ■ (415) 221-5332

This one-of-a-kind store is devoted to old-fashioned hat making. Each hat is custom-made.

5 Aqua Surf Shop
MAP A5 ■ 3847 Judah St ■ (415) 242-9283

Every sort of surf gear, including the extra-thick wetsuits needed to survive these northern waters.

6 Stonestown Galleria
19th Ave & Winston Drive ■ (415) 564-8848

Upmarket Nordstrom and all-purpose Macy's are the anchor stores in this traditional indoor-outdoor shopping center with the usual array of mall stores, from Gap to Sunglass Hut, as well as plenty of food outlets.

7 Green Apple Books
MAP D3 ■ 506 Clement St ■ (415) 387-2272

It's easy to lose a few hours browsing through the selection of used books and DVDs at this store. Part of the fun is taking the time to read the well-written and helpful staff recommendations.

8 Piedmont Boutique
MAP E4 ■ 1452 Haight St ■ (415) 864-8075

A stroll around Haight-Ashbury isn't complete without a visit to Piedmont Boutique, the famous, flashy clothier to the party set for nearly a half-century.

9 Urban Bazaar
MAP D5 ■ 1371 9th Ave between Irving & Judah ■ (415) 664-4422

This cute shop features sustainably made gifts and home decor items, many of them produced locally. The store often hosts local events including craft nights.

10 See's Candies
3250 20th Ave, Stonestown Galleria ■ (415) 731-1784

Founded in 1921 by Charles See, this traditional shop offers high-quality chocolates, truffles, brittles, toffees, and lollipops.

Custom-made hats at Paul's Hat Works

Previous pages Golden Gate Bridge and Fort Point

Places to Eat

PRICE CATEGORIES
For a three-course meal for one with half a bottle of wine (or equivalent meal), taxes, and extra charges.

$ under $40 $$ $40–$80 $$$ over $80

1 Cliff House
MAP A3 ▪ 1090 Point Lobos Ave ▪ (415) 386-3330 ▪ Dis. access ▪ $
Standard American fare, but the real reason to come here is to see the Pacific crashing on the cliffs below and to witness the wonderful sunsets (see p117).

2 Beach Chalet Brewery
MAP A4 ▪ 1000 Great Hwy ▪ (415) 386-8439 ▪ Dis. access ▪ $$
People come here for the views – both of the ocean and the murals – as well as for the food.

3 Kabuto Sushi
MAP C3 ▪ 5121 Geary Blvd at 15th Ave ▪ (415) 752-5652 ▪ Closed Mon ▪ Dis. access ▪ $
A great Japanese restaurant – the sashimi melts in the mouth.

4 Ton Kiang
MAP C3 ▪ 5821 Geary Blvd ▪ (415) 387-8273 ▪ Dis. access ▪ $
Many say this restaurant has the best dim sum on offer in the city. Always fresh, hot, and tasty, with various specialties.

5 Chapeau!
MAP C3 ▪ 126 Clement St at 2nd Ave ▪ (415) 387-0408 ▪ Dis. access ▪ $$$
A memorably authentic French bistro. The sommelier can direct you to fine wines that pair well with the classic fare, which includes roasted pork loin.

6 Outerlands
MAP A3 ▪ 4001 Judah St ▪ (415) 661-6140 ▪ Dis. access ▪ $
The menu changes to reflect the seasons at this popular beachside

Brunch dishes at Outerlands

spot, but fresh baked bread is always on offer. Grab an outside table to watch the world go by, or sit inside and marvel at the reclaimed wood walls.

7 Pizzetta 211
MAP C3 ▪ 211 23rd Ave ▪ (415) 379-9880 ▪ Dis. access ▪ $
Thin and crisp pizza topped with organic ingredients from fragrant aioli to home-made sausage.

8 Q Restaurant
MAP D3 ▪ 225 Clement St ▪ (415) 752-2298 ▪ Dis. access ▪ $$
Friendly staff serve huge portions of comfort food at this local favorite.

9 Java Beach Café
MAP A5 ▪ 1396 La Playa St ▪ (415) 665-5282 ▪ $
This cozy café serves sandwiches, soup, and pastries in a nautical-themed interior.

10 Burma Superstar
MAP D3 ▪ 309 Clement St ▪ (415) 387-2147 ▪ Dis. access ▪ $
This Burmese eatery boasts an extensive menu of flavorsome noodles, curries, and salads.

See map on p116

10 The Bay Area

In local parlance, the Bay Area includes the City, the East Bay, Marin, the Peninsula, and the South Bay. Although Santa Clara, San Jose, Santa Cruz, and Capitola do not touch the waters of the Bay, they embody the same open-minded ethos that defines it. This is probably because the mentality of this swatch of Northern California is so different from that of Southern California. In towns like Berkeley the emphasis is on progressive thinking; smaller enclaves like Bolinas live life in harmony with the breathtaking nature all around them.

Oakland's Paramount

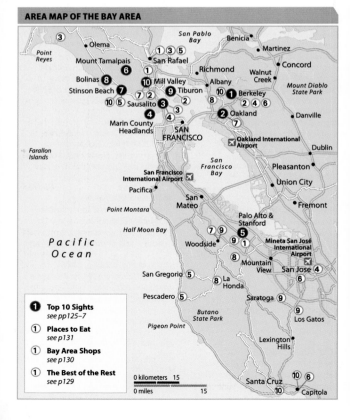

AREA MAP OF THE BAY AREA

- **1** Top 10 Sights
  see pp125–7
- **①** Places to Eat
  see p131
- **①** Bay Area Shops
  see p130
- **①** The Best of the Rest
  see p129

Houseboats in the former fishing community of Sausalito

1 Berkeley
BART Berkeley

Its days as "Berzerkeley," when student protesters and tear-gas clouds filled the streets in the 1960s, are only a fading memory now, although Telegraph Avenue still keeps some of the countercultural traditions alive. A great university, "Cal's" faculty boasts some dozen Nobel laureates, while beautiful parks, tree-lined streets, and unique shops typify this East Bay enclave. Berkeley continues to give more "power to the people" than any other US city, with public services that put other communities to shame.

2 Oakland
BART 12th St

Gertrude Stein's famous dictum about her hometown, that "there is no there there," was challenged by a very proactive mayor, Jerry Brown, from 1997 to 2007 (see p47). Oakland's image – notorious for racial unrest and crime in the past – is being cleaned up to present a more visitor-friendly face, and there has been an influx of creative types who have moved here to flee the high rents of San Francisco. Oakland's attractions include the huge Lake Merritt, which offers a range of recreational possibilities, a beautiful Mormon temple, and its Museum of California (see p128).

3 Sausalito
US 101

A former fishing community and now an upscale commuter area and tourist haven, this small town offers spectacular views of San Francisco from its Bridgeway Avenue promenade. Historically, it has been an artists' town, home to an eccentric mix of residents. Bungalows cling to the hillsides and boats fill the picturesque marinas, many of them houseboats that locals live in year-round. There are excellent restaurants, places to stay, and some unique shopping possibilities, too.

4 Marin County Headlands
Muni Bus 76

To visit these raw, wild hills with astonishingly beautiful views is to enter another world; yet it's only half an hour's drive from the city, by way of the Golden Gate Bridge. The scale of the rolling terrain is immense, and the precipitous drops into the ocean dramatic. This is an unspoiled area of wildlife (Point Reyes to the north is home to tule elk herds), windswept ridges, sheltered valleys, and deserted beaches (see p58).

Tule elk, Marin County Headlands

Stanford University, Palo Alto

⑤ Palo Alto and Stanford
Hwys 101 & 82

An erstwhile sleepy university town, Palo Alto has experienced a boom as the focal point of Silicon Valley, and driving force of the "New Economy." Although a lot of the gilding has lately fallen off the lily, this town has been left with a considerably dressed-up appearance, as well as many fancy restaurants, hotels, and shops. The town is home to prestigious private Stanford University, with its beautiful, well-tended campus (see p65).

GREAT BAY AREA UNIVERSITIES

Palo Alto's Stanford University is the Bay Area's most famous private institution of higher learning, inaugurated in 1891. However, in terms of intellectual clout, the University of California at Berkeley, the oldest campus in the California system, stands shoulder to shoulder, considering the number of Nobel laureates on the faculty and its international importance. Stanford is known for business, law, and medicine, Berkeley for law, engineering, and nuclear physics. Both universities are among the most selective in the country.

---

⑥ Mount Tamalpais
Hwy 1

From the summit of 2,570-ft (785-m) "Mount Tam," sacred to the Native Americans who once lived here, practically the entire Bay Area can be seen. The area is a state park, with more than 200 miles (320 km) of trails through redwood groves and alongside creeks. There are picnic areas, campsites, an open-air theater, and meadows for kite flying.

Mountain Theatre, Mount Tamalpais

⑦ Stinson Beach
Hwy 1

Since the early 20th century, this has been a popular vacation spot and remains the preferred swimming beach for the whole area (see p58). The soft sand and the spectacular sunsets set off the quaint village, with its good restaurants and interesting shops. You can reach it via the coast route, but the drive up Highway 1 gives the most dramatic arrival, with inspiring views as you exit the forest onto the headlands.

8 Bolinas
Hwy 1

Bolinas is a hippie village that time forgot. The citizens regularly take down road signs showing the way to their special place, to keep away visitors. Potters and other crafts-people sell their wares in the funky gallery, organic produce and vegetarianism are the rule, and 1960s idealism still predominates.

"Ark Row" shops, Tiburon

9 Tiburon
Hwy 131

Marin County's less hectic alternative to Sausalito – here, 100-year-old houseboats ("arks") have been pulled ashore and refurbished, forming "Ark Row," with shops, restaurants, and cafés that enhance the charm of this waterfront village. There are also opportunities to see wildlife in the parks along the shore, facing Angel Island and the city.

10 Mill Valley
Off Hwy 101

Home to a well-known film festival, this is the quintessential Marin town; wealthy, relaxed, beautiful, and with a well-educated populace given to liberal views on just about every topic. The old part of town is flanked by redwoods, lined with old buildings that house restaurants and unusual shops, and the whole centers around an eternally pleasant public square.

A MORNING WALK AROUND BERKELEY

▶ Begin at the **UC Berkeley University Visitor Center** at 101 Sproul Hall near the intersection of Bancroft Way and Telegraph Avenue, where you can pick up information and maps. Follow around to University Drive and on to the university campus, passing Romanesque **Wellman Hall**, then take a left on Cross Campus Road. Straight ahead is the main campus landmark, the 307-ft (94-m) **Sather Tower**, also known simply as the Campanile, based on the famous bell tower in Venice's Piazza San Marco.

Now continue on to rejoin University Drive and go around to the **Hearst Greek Theater**, venue for excellent concerts of all sorts. Next, head for handsome Sather Gate, which leads into **Sproul Plaza**, epicenter of the student Free Speech Movement protests that erupted into almost nonstop sociopolitical unrest in the 1960s and 1970s.

Exit the campus onto Telegraph Avenue, a kind of East Bay Haight-Ashbury with radical vibes all its own, and once home of the legendary bookstore Cody's, controversially closed in 2008. One block over is idealistic **People's Park**. Continue on back to Bancroft Way to pay a visit to the **University Art Museum** and the **Pacific Film Archive**.

After your walk, head over to **The Cheese Board Collective** (1512 Shattuck Ave at Vine St; (510) 549-3183). The restaurant serves home-made vegetarian pizzas with creative toppings such as asparagus, Gouda, and gremolata.

See map on p124 ◀

Oakland Museum of California

1 The Building
The museum building is an outstanding example of modern design. Opened in 1969, it is composed of reinforced concrete and consists of three levels of tiered terraces. To soften the angularity, roof gardens have been planted, accented with sculpture.

Oakland Museum of California

2 Natural Sciences
In the brilliant Natural Sciences Department, the state of California is presented as one of the world's top ten biological "hot spots." There are thousands of artifacts on display, including bird and mammal study skins and mounts, as well as an enormous collection of reptiles, amphibians, and fungi.

3 Gold Rush Artifacts
The lives of those who came to California from all over the world in the 19th century, hoping to strike it rich, are chronicled here. You'll see gold nuggets, prospecting tools and rare mining equipment.

Gold nugget

4 Mission-era Artifacts
A 19th-century icon of St. Peter is just one remnant of the Spanish Mission years you'll find here, where there are also colonial tools, and part of a Spanish ship.

5 The Earliest Californians
Fascinating galleries explore early human history in the state of California, documented by materials such as basketry, stone tools, clothing, and objects used in rituals.

6 Earthquake Artifacts
A collection of objects that pertain to the terrible earthquake of 1906 are on display here, including porcelain cups and saucers fused together by the heat of the fire that destroyed so much of the city.

7 Californian History
This section of the museum has exhibits associated with technology, agriculture, business, and domestic life from the early Native Americans up to the 21st century. Subjects such as World War II, baby boomers, Hollywood, and Silicon Valley are also covered.

8 Art Gallery
The third level of the museum is devoted to the Gallery of California Art, featuring works by artists who have studied, lived, and worked here. Included are works by California Impressionists and members of the Bay Area Figurative Movement. Check the website (museumca.org) for the opening times of the California Art and History Galleries.

9 Photography
The Gallery of California Art also has an impressive collection of the work of California photographers, including Ansel Adams, Edward Weston, and Dorothea Lange.

10 Californian Crafts
This is the largest collection in the world of work by California Arts and Crafts practitioners Arthur and Lucia Kleinhans Mathews, including paintings, drawings, furniture, and other decorative art.

The Best of the Rest

1 San Rafael
Hwy 101

This town has a charming historic center with good restaurants and shops. A street market transforms the main drag into a bustling hub every Thursday evening.

2 Belvedere Island
This garden island, attached by a causeway to Tiburon, is one of the Bay's most exclusive residential areas. Worth a visit to see the palatial homes and their sumptuous setting.

3 Point Reyes
Hwy 1 to Olema, then signposted to Point Reyes

This windswept peninsula is a haven for wildlife, including a herd of tule elk; it is also home to cattle ranches. You can watch migrating whales offshore from December to March.

4 San Jose
Hwy 101

This sprawling town is an integral part of Silicon Valley enterprises and has popular attractions.

5 San Gregorio and Pescadero
Hwy 1

San Gregorio, protected by cliffs, is the Bay Area's oldest nudist beach. Pescadero, as well as having a state beach with wonderful tide pools, is a lovely town that looks like something out of the Old West, complete with a whitewashed wooden church. The thriving farming community produces asparagus and pumpkins.

Lighthouse, Pescadero

6 Winchester Mystery House
525 S Winchester Blvd, San Jose ▪ (408) 247-2101 ▪ Open daily (call for tour times) ▪ Adm

The eccentric 19th-century home of the rifle heiress, Sarah Winchester, took 38 years to build and includes stairways leading to nowhere and windows set into floors.

Winchester Mystery House

7 Woodside
Hwy 280

This bucolic residential area is where many of the first families to have lived in the Bay Area built fabulous mansions in the late 19th century.

8 La Honda and Old La Honda Roads
Off Hwy 280

The most picturesque way to make the approach to the tiny community of La Honda and the scenic Skyline Boulevard (see p119) is via the switchbacks of these two roads.

9 Los Gatos and Saratoga
Hwy 280

These outpost towns still retain some frontier atmosphere, although they are now communities for the movers and shakers of Silicon Valley.

10 Santa Cruz and Capitola
Hwy 1

Some of the Central Coast's best swimming, plus the Boardwalk, a famous vintage amusement park.

See map on p124

Shops

1 Stanford Shopping Center
606 Stanford Shopping Center, Palo Alto ▪ Hwy 101 ▪ (650) 617-8200

One of the first shopping centers in the Bay Area, this outdoor mall is dog-friendly and features shops that you don't tend to find everywhere, such as Kate Spade, Free People, and Bloomingdales.

2 Powell's Sweet Shoppe
3206 College Ave, Berkeley ▪ Hwy 80 ▪ (510) 658-9866

This old-fashioned candy store features row upon row of brightly colored gummy candies, chocolates, and lollipops, plus a number of vintage penny candies and novelty confectionery, such as bacon soda.

Candy at Powell's Sweet Shoppe

3 Gene Hiller
729 Bridgeway Ave, Sausalito ▪ Hwy 101 ▪ (415) 332-3636

For over 50 years, this menswear store has been offering the finest imported designer clothing – from classic formal to casual – including Ermenegildo Zegna and Canali.

4 Global Exchange
2840 College Ave, Berkeley ▪ Hwy 80 ▪ (510) 548-0370

Beautiful handmade creations from such places as Vietnam, Indonesia, Mexico, and Senegal. The producers receive most of the profits.

Handmade products, Global Exchange

5 Via Diva
516 Irwin St, San Rafael ▪ Off Hwy 101 ▪ (415) 257-8881

This broad collection of art and artifacts includes treasures from China, Indonesia, India, Thailand, and South America.

6 Treehouse Green Gifts
2935 College Ave, Berkeley ▪ Hwy 80 ▪ (510) 204-9292

This eco-friendly store sells home accessories, garden items, and gifts for babies and kids, all produced by unique artists.

7 Tyler Florence Shop
59 Throckmorton Rd, Mill Valley ▪ Off Hwy 101 ▪ (415) 380 9200

The flagship store of local celebrity chef Tyler Florence stocks everything from home-made granola to specialty pepper mills.

8 Convert
1844 4th St, Berkeley ▪ Hwy 101 ▪ (510) 984-0142

This trendy boutique, selling clothes and shoes for men and women, focuses on sustainably sourced lines.

9 Shady Lane
325 Sharon Park Drive, Menlo Park ▪ (650) 321-1099

This boutique was founded by a collective of artists who wanted to create a showcase for their designs in areas like jewelry and ceramics.

10 Claudia Chapline Gallery and Sculpture Garden
3445 Shoreline Hwy, Stinson Beach ▪ Hwy 1 ▪ (415) 868-2308

In a great setting near the beach, the Chapline sculpture garden is full of delights, especially the brilliant kinetic pieces driven by the wind, which are the work of Lyman Whitaker. Inside, the variety and quality of painted and mixed-media work is very compelling.

Places to Eat

PRICE CATEGORIES
For a three-course meal for one with half a bottle of wine (or equivalent meal), taxes, and extra charges.
....
$ under $40 **$$** $40–$80 **$$$** over $80

1 Tony Tutto Pizza
246 East Blithedale Ave, Mill Valley ▪ Hwy 101 & Hwy 1 ▪ (415) 283-8646 ▪ Dis. access ▪ $
Crispy thin-crust pizzas made with fresh organic ingredients. Most of the tables are outside, so it can get quite cramped if the weather is bad.

2 Vasco
106 Throckmorton Ave, Mill Valley ▪ Hwy 101 & Hwy 1 ▪ (415) 381-3343 ▪ Closed L ▪ $
Vasco serves delicious pizzas, pastas, and desserts. The downside is there's often a wait for a table.

3 Sol Food Puerto Rican Cuisine
901 Lincoln Ave, San Rafael ▪ Hwy 101 ▪ (415) 451-4765 ▪ $
Locals and tourists alike line up for a taste of the flavorful, festive food at this bright green restaurant.

4 The Bridgeway Café
633 Bridgeway, Sausalito ▪ Hwy 101 ▪ (415) 332-3426 ▪ Dis. access ▪ $
You'll find a range of American favorites at this cozy little diner looking onto the Bay.

5 Parkside Snack Bar
43 Arenal Ave, Stinson Beach ▪ Hwy 1 ▪ (415) 868-1272 ▪ Dis. access ▪ $
Creative brunch at picnic tables on the patio, or in the dining room. Try the Tomales Bay mussels in curry.

6 Gayle's
504 Bay Ave, Capitola ▪ Hwy 1 ▪ (831) 462-1200 ▪ Dis. access ▪ $
This bakery and *rosticceria* (or deli) features an extraordinary selection of

A selection of cakes at Gayle's

gourmet treats, both sweet and savory. Try the cappucino cake and the to-die-for cupcakes.

7 Café Eritrea d'Afrique
4069 Telegraph Ave, Oakland ▪ Hwy 880 ▪ (510) 547-4520 ▪ $
An acclaimed restaurant serving Eritrean and Ethiopian cuisine in a relaxing and friendly atmosphere. They offer an all-you-can-eat veggie buffet on Wednesdays and Fridays.

8 Alpine Inn
3915 Alpine Rd, Portola Valley ▪ Hwy 280 ▪ (650) 854-4004 ▪ Dis. access ▪ $
In a building that dates back to 1850, this greasy beer bar with a garden is popular with locals and Silicon Valley workers alike for its substantial burgers and fries.

9 Buck's
3062 Woodside Drive, Woodside ▪ Hwy 280 ▪ (650) 851-8010 ▪ Dis. access ▪ $
After a long hike on one of the many trails in Woodside, enjoy a hearty Woodside omelet and coffee at this kitsch restaurant.

10 Chez Panisse
1517 Shattuck Ave, Berkeley ▪ Hwy 80 ▪ (510) 548-5525 ▪ Closed Sun ▪ $$$
A popular Berkeley spot which has been serving up excellent California cuisine since 1971. The upstairs café offers a cheaper alternative.

See map on p124

Streetsmart

**The crooked turns of
Lombard Street**

Getting To and Around San Francisco

Arriving by Air

Three international airports serve the San Francisco Bay Area, all linked by public transportation to one another. **San Francisco International Airport** (SFO) is 14 miles (23 km) south of the city. It is one of the busiest airports on Earth, with over 40 airlines from around the world operating here. However, it is also one of the most user-friendly.

The airport's **Bay Area Rapid Transit** (BART) station is connected to the terminals by a light-rail shuttle (although it stops frequently, so allow time for the journey). BART connects to four Downtown stations, and to **Caltrain**, which connects to San Jose.

Rental cars, taxis, limousines, and shuttles to surrounding cities and Downtown hotels are available at the airport. There are some minibus companies, such as **BayPorter Express** and **American Airporter Shuttle**, that offer a door-to-door shuttle service, taking passengers to a specific address. The cost of the trip is shared with the other passengers. A taxi ride from SFO into the city averages at about $50 plus tip.

Oakland International Airport (OAK) is a half-hour **AC Transit** bus ride across the Bay from San Francisco. There is good transportation into San Francisco by door-to-door bus, car, and limousine shuttle services. The airport is served by BART in conjunction with a shuttle, getting passengers into the city within an hour.

Mineta San Jose International Airport (SJC), in the heart of Silicon Valley, is 45 miles (72 km) south of San Francisco. **SamTrans** provides a 24-hour bus service to the city and San Mateo County. BART and Caltrain also provide transport from SJC into San Francisco.

Arriving by Bus

Greyhound buses arrive in the city from across the country to the station at 200 Folsom Street. The most affordable but time-consuming way to cover long distances in the US, buses usually have power outlets and free Wi-Fi.

Arriving by Train

Amtrak trains access San Francisco from stations across the country. The closest station is Emeryville, to the north of Oakland. Amtrak runs a free shuttle to the city center.

Arriving by Sea

Cruise ships dock at Pier 35, which is the embarkation and debarkation point of many Alaskan or Mexican Riviera cruises. Taxis and modes of public transportation are available at the dock.

Traveling by Bus, Muni Metro, and Cable Car

The San Francisco Municipal Transportation Agency, or **Muni** as it is commonly called, runs the city buses, Muni Metro light rail, cable cars, and streetcars. Purchase money- and time-saving Muni passports, which can be used on all the above modes of transport.

As much tourist attraction as transportation, **cable cars** and vintage streetcars trundle in style around city streets. The world-famous cable cars run between Market Street and Fisherman's Wharf, on the north–south Powell-Mason and Powell-Hyde lines, and on the east–west California Street line.

Bay Area Rapid Transit (BART)

BART operates five fast routes to dozens of stations throughout the city. Running from 4am to 11:45pm, three or four trains are scheduled per hour, with more during peak commuting times.

Transport Passes

The **Clipper** card gives passengers access to all participating Bay Area transport, including Muni (except cable cars) and BART, with an easy-to-use, reloadable card that is good for 90 days. Purchase them at Muni vending machines in subway stations and at many retailers. Muni tickets can also be purchased for single or round-trip rides, and reloaded as needed. Just tap the card or ticket at the Clipper reader upon entering a faregate or boarding a vehicle. **CityPass** saves up to 47 per cent on unlimited cable car and Muni rides, plus admission to four city attractions.

By Taxi and Ride Services

Taxis are easy to get at the airport, but often hard to catch in the city, even when you call for them; the best chance is from a major Downtown hotel. **Uber** and **Lyft** are popular ride services that pick passengers up efficiently wherever they are in the city. You order your ride and then pay for it, both by cell phone.

By Car

Many visitors leave their cars at their lodgings, as expensive parking garages, sparse street parking, and congestion can make driving frustrating and time-consuming, even in this small, compact city. Reliable car rental agencies include **Hertz**, **SFO Rental Car Center**, and **Zipcar**.

By Bicycle

In this bicycle-friendly city, there are miles of designated lanes and parking spaces, as well as easy bicycle transport options on public transportation. SFO has a station where riders can disassemble or assemble their bicycles, and boxes available for checking bicycles in as luggage (see **SFO Bike Information**). For cycling routes and further information, see **SF Bicycle Coalition**.

By Ferry

A breezy way to get around the Bay Area is by the many passenger ferries that arrive at Fisherman's Wharf and the Ferry Building from Marin County and the East Bay, such as **Golden Gate Ferry** and **San Francisco Bay Ferry**. From the Ferry Building at the foot of Market Street, myriad public transportation is available. **Blue and Gold Fleet** offers bay cruises.

DIRECTORY

AIRPORTS

Mineta San Jose International Airport
(408) 392-3600
w flysanjose.com

Oakland International Airport
(510) 563-3300
w oaklandairport.com

San Francisco International Airport
(650) 821-8211
w flysfo.com

BUSES, MUNI METRO AND CABLE CAR

AC Transit
w actransit.org

American Airporter Shuttle
w americanairporter.com

BayPorter Express
w bayporter.com

Greyhound
w greyhound.com

Muni
w sfmta.com

SamTrans
w samtrans.com

RAIL

Amtrak
w amtrak.com

Bay Area Rapid Transit
w bart.gov

Cable Cars
w sfcablecar.com

Caltrain
w caltrain.com

TRANSPORT PASSES

CityPass
w citypass.com

Clipper
w clippercard.com

RIDE SERVICES

Lyft
w lyft.com

Uber
w uber.com

CAR RENTAL

Hertz
w hertz.com

SFO Rental Car Center
w flysfo.com

Zipcar
w zipcar.com

BICYCLES

SF Bicycle Coalition
w sfbike.org

SFO Bike Information
w flysfo.com/to-from/biking

FERRIES

Blue and Gold Fleet
w blueandgoldfleet.com

Golden Gate Ferry
w goldengateferry.org

San Francisco Bay Ferry
w sanfranciscobayferry.com

Practical Information

Passports and Visas

All travelers to the US need a valid passport. Most European citizens, as well as citizens from Australia, New Zealand, and Japan, need a non-refundable return ticket from outside the US to qualify for the Visa Waiver Program (VWP), which allows citizens of participating countries to enter the US without a visa for stays of 90 days or less. The **Electronic System for Travel Authorization** is an automated system that determines visitors' eligibility for the VWP.

Other nationalities must secure a visa from a US consulate or embassy before traveling. All major countries have consulates in San Francisco; for questions about visiting, contact your national representative.

Customs Regulations

You are allowed to bring in 1.75 pints (1 liter) of wine or liquor, 200 cigarettes, 100 cigars, 3 lb (1.3 kg) of tobacco, and $100 worth of gifts. Some items are not allowed, such as certain fruits and vegetables, animals, and animal products. You may carry up to $10,000 in US or foreign currency out of or into the country; larger sums must be declared, which entails filing form CM 4790. See the **US Customs and Border Protection** website for details.

Travel Insurance

Travel insurance is invaluable when you need to cancel a trip because of illness, death of a relative, weather, or emergency medical care and evacuation, as well as to cover lost baggage or canceled flights. **Insure My Trip** sells travel coverage from several carriers; you enter your trip details and your needs in order to receive several quotes. **Europ Assistance USA** offers multilingual, 24-hour assistance including medical evacuation, emergency cash, help with lost documents and baggage, and medical case management. Travelers from EEA countries should carry their European Health Insurance Card (EHIC), which covers only "necessary medical treatment."

Health

No vaccinations are required for foreign visitors to the US. San Francisco has several major hospitals, including **Saint Francis Memorial Hospital**, **Davies Medical Center**, and **San Francisco General Hospital**. For minor medical issues, walk-in clinics are found throughout the city, including **Care Practice** and **Traveler Medical Group**. Expect to pay for any type of healthcare that you receive; often you will be asked to arrange for payment before the treatment. Confirm in advance that the hospital or clinic accepts your insurance coverage. Pharmacies are located within most large chain supermarkets.

Unsafe sex is frowned upon in this gay-friendly city. The drop-in **San Francisco City Clinic** provides free or low-cost diagnosis and treatment of STDs, plus free condoms, emergency contraception, and post-exposure prevention.

Personal Security

Dial 911 for real emergencies, and have your information and location ready. As in all cities, when parking, you should remove or stash valuables out of sight and lock your car. Patronize parking garages that have attendants on duty. Take care with your belongings while sitting at sidewalk tables and in crowds. Be alert after dark in the Lower Haight, the Mission, Golden Gate Park, and Fisherman's Wharf, and in the Tenderloin. For personal items lost on Muni, contact **Muni Lost and Found**. For contact details of the **SFO Lost and Found**, see the airport's website.

Tourist Information

The **San Francisco Visitor Information Center** is loaded with information, coupons, tour tickets, and money-saving passes for visitors to the city. Well in advance of your arrival, check out the website with its "trip ideas" and "deals" sections, and calendar of events. You can also use it to book hotels and request a free Visitor's Guide by mail or download a digital version. At the center itself, you can pick up CityPasses, Muni passports, and maps, and make use of the Wi-Fi and computers for free.

Gay and Lesbian Travelers

One of the most gay-friendly cities in the world, San Francisco offers plenty of LGBT-welcoming hotels and nightspots, particularly in the lively Castro district where many gay residents live. The organizer of the largest annual event in the city, the Pride Celebration and Parade, **San Francisco Pride** publishes an online calendar of events of interest to LGBT visitors. The **LGBT Center** is also a great source of information.

Disabled Travelers

Disabled access is extensive throughout the city, from ramped curbs to telecommunication devices for hearing-impaired travelers. Discounted fares for disabled passengers are available on all transit. The free **Muni Access Guide** is available on the Muni website, and gives pointers on how to make the most of the system. Some Muni buses hydraulically assist wheelchair-bound people to board and be secured.

Access Northern California provides information on accessible travel and recreation throughout the region. National parks offer free admission for disabled and fellow passengers in the same vehicle, and many city attractions offer reduced entrance fees. The San Francisco Visitor Information Center publishes the free Access San Francisco Guide.

Disabled-accessible toilets are provided in many places, including hotels and restaurants, main city attractions, and public buildings.

DIRECTORY

PASSPORTS AND VISAS

Australian Consulate General
MAP P5 ▪ 576 Market St
((415) 644-3620

British Consulate General
MAP P5 ▪ 1 Sansome St
((415) 617-1300

Canadian Consulate General
MAP N5 ▪ 580 California St
((415) 834-3180

Electronic System for Travel Authorization
ⓦ cbp.gov

CUSTOMS

US Customs and Border Protection
ⓦ cbp.gov

TRAVEL INSURANCE

Europ Assistance USA
ⓦ worldwideassistance.com

Insure My Trip
ⓦ insuremytrip.com

HEALTH SERVICES

Care Practice
MAP F4 ▪ 508 14th St
((415) 864-4444

Davies Medical Center
MAP E4 ▪ 45 Castro St
((415) 565-6060

Saint Francis Memorial Hospital
MAP N2 ▪ 900 Hyde St
((415) 353-6300

San Francisco City Clinic
MAP G4 ▪ 356 7th St
((415) 487-5500

San Francisco General Hospital
MAP G5 ▪ 1001 Potrero Ave
((415) 206-8000

Traveler Medical Group
MAP P3 ▪ 490 Post St
((415) 963-4398

PERSONAL SECURITY

Emergency Services
(911

Muni Lost and Found
(311 or (415) 701 2311

SFO Lost and Found
ⓦ flysfo.com

TOURIST INFORMATION

San Francisco Visitor Information Center
MAP Q3 ▪ 900 Market St
ⓦ sanfrancisco.travel

GAY AND LESBIAN TRAVELERS

LGBT Center
ⓦ sfcenter.org

San Francisco Pride
ⓦ sfpride.org

DISABLED TRAVELERS

Access Northern California
ⓦ accessnca.org

Muni Access Guide
ⓦ sfmta.com

Currency and Banking

US bank notes come in denominations of $1, $5, $10, $20, $50, and $100. Coins are 1c, 5c (nickel), 10c (dime), 25c (quarter), and the less common 50c and $1. Currency exchange is available at the three international airports, at Downtown banks and hotels, and at **Travelex America**. ATMs are the best way to get cash. To avoid the fees added to ATM transactions, make a purchase in a store and ask for cash. Debit cards are accepted for every transaction type.

Travelers' checks are no longer widely accepted, even sometimes by the banks that issue them. Without a credit card, you will not be able to rent a car or check into a hotel. Visa and MasterCard are accepted everywhere, while Discover and Diners Club cards are often refused, and even American Express may be refused at smaller businesses.

Postal Services

Most US post offices are open from 9am to 5:30pm Monday to Friday and from 9am to 2pm on Saturdays. The **Union Square Post Office** is centrally located. Stamps are also available at some hotels, chain supermarkets and drugstores.

Telephone and Internet

San Francisco's area code is 415: omit this when calling within the city. Surrounding cities have other area codes: you dial 1 followed by the area code. Toll-free numbers start with 800, 877, 888, or similar prefixes. Dial 411 to get local and national numbers. International calls should be preceded by 011. To save money, buy a phone card or a cheap cellphone. Cellphones can also be rented from **InTouch USA**.

Wi-Fi is free at the airports and at cafés and lodgings. You can also access free Wi-Fi in public spaces by connecting to #SFWiFi. Find more hot spots at the **Open WiFi Spots** website. Computers are available to use for free at the San Francisco Visitor Information Center and libraries.

Newspapers, Magazines, TV, and Radio

Besides publishing a daily newspaper, the *San Francisco Chronicle* maintains a website of news, events, performing arts, restaurant and movie reviews, and travel tips and articles. Light-hearted, liberal, and free, *SF Weekly* covers the arts, events, and eateries, in print and online. Both free, the *Bay Area Reporter* and *San Francisco Bay Times* cater to the LGBT community. *San Francisco Magazine* and *7x7* are urban-lifestyle print and online publications covering topics such as fashion, entertainment, culture, and food in the Bay Area.

The Bay Area hosts every major TV and radio network. For local news, traffic, and weather, tune into **KGO** TV and radio.

Opening Hours

Shops are generally open daily from 10am to 5pm or later. Some groceries, drugstores, and super-markets are open daily from 7am to 11pm. Chain stores and malls are often open on holidays.

Banks are open from 9am to 5pm Monday to Friday, and many are open on Saturdays. Museums and attractions have their own hours; most are open daily.

Time Difference

The US is divided into four time zones, with San Francisco in the Pacific Standard Time zone. It's 3 hours behind New York and 8 hours behind London. Daylight Saving Time moves the clock one hour ahead from the second Sunday in March until the first Sunday in November.

Electrical Appliances

The US uses 110–120 volts AC. If your appliances use 220–240 volts (as in most of Europe), bring a 110-volt transformer and a plug adapter with two flat parallel pins.

Driving

Foreign drivers' licenses are recognized in the US. Take care to notice parking signs; parking tickets are expensive and towing fees run into hundreds of dollars. When you park in this hilly city pointing uphill, turn your wheels toward the center of the street; when ointing downhill, turn our wheels toward the sidewalk. After coming to a complete stop, you can turn right at a red light after yielding to traffic and pedestrians. Watch carefully for the ubiquitous one-way streets.

All passengers must wear seat belts. Infants from 0–1 years must be in the backseat in a rear-facing car seat until they reach 20 lb (9 kg). Children under 8 must be secured in a car seat or booster seat in the backseat. Those 4 ft 9 inches (1.5 m) or taller may be secured by a safety belt in the backseat. If your child does not have a car seat, you may be denied boarding a van or taxi, or stopped by police while driving and fined $100–250. For rental cars, reserve your car seat(s) when booking the vehicle.

Weather

The Pacific marine climate means mild year-round weather, with temperatures seldom rising above 70° F (21° C) or falling below 40° F (5° C). Bring layers – evenings are nearly always cool, and fog can roll in any day, especially in the summer time.

Natural Disasters

As major fault lines are found throughout the San Francisco Bay Area, earthquakes do occur from time to time. The biggest danger is from things falling, so if you are inside, do not run outside where there are street signs, traffic lights, power

lines, and trees. Stay calm and move away from windows and mirrors. If you are in bed, lie on the floor next to the mattress. In a minute or so, the tremors should stop. Smaller aftershocks may ensue. Californians know that to be ready for any natural disaster, they should have enough supplies to last 72 hours.

Shopping

One of the most expensive shopping cities in the world, San Francisco also has plenty of ethnic neighborhoods where bargains and souvenirs can be had. High-end department stores and designer boutiques cluster around Union Square, while antiques shops and fine art galleries line up at Jackson Square. Union and Chestnut Streets are window-shoppers' meccas. There are vintage, boutique, and ethnic stores, galleries, and crafts emporiums to be discovered on Fillmore and Haight Streets and in Hayes Valley. In the Mission District, both funky fashion and Latino-style decor and apparel can be found. Chinatown and Japantown attract tourists after Asian trinkets and souvenirs.

The massive, upscale Westfield San Francisco Center is on Market Street (see p79) and Crocker Galleria lures fashionistas and Downtown office workers (see p78). Embarcadero Center on the waterfront is a four-block-square, high-rise complex of more than 100 shops and

restaurants (see p79). At Fisherman's Wharf, indoor/outdoor malls cater to visitors with restaurants, live entertainment, and boutique and souvenir stores. Other malls include Ghirardelli Square (see p79), The Cannery (see p17), Anchorage Shopping Center (see p16), and Pier 39 (see p16).

Dining

San Francisco has more restaurants per capita than any other US city and chefs are celebrities in this town of foodies. Reflecting the city's cultural diversity, eateries run the gamut from Mexican *taquerías* to Italian pasta houses, from Chinatown's dim sum parlors to sushi bars in Japantown, and from all-American diners to some of the best French restaurants outside Europe. The Bay Area was the birthplace of California Cuisine, an approach to fresh, seasonal, local ingredients, and dramatic presentation that changed American restaurant fare forever. Many of the trendy restaurants in the city are melding California Cuisine with the exotic tastes of Southeast Asia, China, and Japan, a combination called Asian Fusion. Locals love their neighborhood Thai, Indian, Chinese, and Italian restaurants where they can fill up without having to empty their wallets.

Pacific Ocean seafood tops the menus throughout the city: fresh-caught Dungeness crab, Petrale sole, Point Reyes oysters and clams, calamari, rock cod, and wild salmon. The fresh seafood available in the city makes for tasty *cioppino* (a fish stew that originated here), clam chowder, and mixed grills. Although Fisherman's Wharf restaurants are pricey, some of the long-established places, such as Scoma's (see p101),

offer good value, and serve legendary seafood right off their own boats.

With the city's high-tech economy on the rise, menu prices are rising, too. Fortunately, the city is also loaded with reasonably priced ethnic restaurants, neighborhood bistros, and deli cafés. Savvy travelers order the prix-fixe specials, eat tapas in bars during happy hour, and check out food trucks in the weekly **Off the Grid** market gatherings. Excellent restaurant reviews, ranging from elegant to affordable eateries and covering every type of ethnic variety, can be found on the **SF Gate** website. These reviews are also searchable by neighborhood. **Tablehopper** offers a free weekly column about the San Francisco dining scene. At the most famous restaurants in the city, reservations are a must, often days or even weeks in advance. **OpenTable** makes it easy to browse restaurants by type, location, and availability, then make reservations online.

Trips and Tours

Taking an organized trip or tour is a popular way to get around and see as much of the city and its surrounding areas as possible. The choice of such tours is plentiful. **Big Bus San Francisco** offers multilingual, hop-on-hop-off, open-top bus tours of the main attractions of the city, as does **Duck Tours**, which then splash into the Bay for a cruise to McCovey Cove. **San Francisco Whale Tours** sail under the Golden Gate Bridge to a vast Marine Sanctuary to see whales and sea turtles. **Alcatraz Cruises** offer narrated ferry rides and multilingual audio walking tour of the island. For free walking tours of the city led by savvy locals and historians, try **San Francisco City Guides**. For on-foot explorations of the Presidio, hidden stairways, urban forests, and hilly neighborhoods, **Urban Hiker San Francisco** is a good bet. **Edible Excursions** offers culinary strolls through Ferry Building Marketplace, the Mission District and Japantown, as well as seasonal trips to West Marin. The tour guides offer insight into the culinary background of each area, with stops along the way to taste samples.

Where to Stay

In recent years, San Francisco has seen many of its older properties transformed into themed boutique hotels, with examples including the rock-and-roll-themed Phoenix Hotel (see p146), the literary hideaway of the Hotel Rex (see p142), and the Beaux Arts landmark Hotel Monaco (see p142).

A precious trove of the city's Victorian mansions now serve as splendid B&Bs. **Bed & Breakfast San Francisco** lists carefully selected private residences open to guests in every desirable neighborhood of San Francisco, including Pacific Heights and the

Marina, as well as farther afield in Marin County and the Wine Country.

Updated grand hotels, originally built before or shortly after the 1906 earthquake, are popular with visitors wanting an authentic San Francisco experience: the Fairmont, (see p144) the Westin St. Francis (see p144), the Palace Hotel (see p144), and the InterContinental Mark Hopkins (see p145) are all good choices.

In this international trading center and major convention city, high-rise hotels cater to a business clientele (which makes up more than a third of all hotel guests) with state-of-the-art electronics, multilingual staff, private voicemail, and commodious work spaces. Solo female travelers like the extra-secure "club" floors with separate elevators, private lounges and conference rooms, and complimentary food and drink, the better to entertain and meet with business colleagues. Over half of the lodgings in the city are within walking distance of the gigantic Moscone Center convention complex (see p32).

In one of the most popular cities in the world for tourism and business, hotels fill up during holidays, in the summer, and when big conventions are in town (which is often). Flexibility on dates is recommended, and to save money on accommodation, savvy visitors book hotels away from Fisherman's Wharf and Union Square, seeking bargains around the Civic Center, the Marina, Japantown, SoMa and Haight-Ashbury.

Parking is limited and expensive – most hotels charge $20–$50 to park overnight. Hotel breakfasts can be pricey, too, so if you see a deal that includes both, it is wise to grab it. B&Bs and smaller properties with fewer amenities can be around half the price of four-star hotels.

The cheapest stays, especially for families, are in dormitory-style rooms in hostels (see p148); private family rooms are also available. Hostels have common kitchens and laundry facilities, but bring your own linens or sleeping bags. Book well ahead, as California hostels are very popular. **Hostelling International** has a good selection on its website.

Headquartered in San Francisco and a popular choice of accommodation in nearly 200 countries, **Airbnb** connects home- and apartment-owners with travelers on a budget. The accommodations and their owners are user-reviewed on the website. Renting a room or an entire house from a local saves money and comes with invaluable insider advice and a friendly welcome. **Vacation Rentals by Owner** (VRBO) offers a similar service, while **Home Exchange** and **Invented City** allow homeowners to trade their homes at a time that is convenient to both parties.

DIRECTORY

DINING

Off the Grid
W offthegridsf.com

OpenTable
W opentable.com

SF Gate
W sfgate.com

Tablehopper
W tablehopper.com

TRIPS AND TOURS

Alcatraz Cruises
W alcatrazcruises.com

Big Bus San Francisco
W eng.bigbustours.com

Duck Tours
W sanfranciscoduck.com

Edible Excursions
W edibleexcursions.net

San Francisco City Guides
W sfcityguides.org

San Francisco Whale Tours
W sanfranciscowhale tours.com

Urban Hiker San Francisco
W urbanhikersf.com

WHERE TO STAY

Airbnb
W airbnb.com

Bed & Breakfast San Francisco
W bbsf.com

Home Exchange
W homeexchange.com

Hostelling International
W norcalhostels.org

Invented City
W invented-city.com

Vacation Rentals by Owner
W vrbo.com

Places to Stay

PRICE CATEGORIES
For a standard, double room per night (with breakfast if included), taxes, and extra charges.

$ under $200 $$ $200–$300 $$$ over $300

Boutique Hotels

Hotel Triton
MAP P4 ▪ 342 Grant Ave ▪ (415) 394-0500 ▪ www. hoteltriton.com ▪ Dis. access ▪ $
Perhaps the city's most original hotel, featuring avant-garde touches – evening tarot card readings, feather boa rental, and several suites designed by rock celebrities, including Jerry Garcia of the Grateful Dead fame. It's all too cool for words; you might run into Cher or Courtney Love, both of whom have stayed here.

Mill Valley Inn
165 Throckmorton Ave, Mill Valley ▪ (415) 389-6608 ▪ www.marinhotels. com ▪ $
Combining the sophistication of a European hotel – tea is served all day – with the cozy charm of a Californian mill town, this intimate option is tucked away in a redwood grove.

The Clift
MAP P3 ▪ 495 Geary St ▪ (415) 775-4700 ▪ www. morganshotelgroup.com ▪ Dis. access ▪ $$
Possessing "equal parts wit, surrealism, and glamour." the proprietors of this Ian Schrager property, offer interior design by Philippe Starck. You'll laugh with delight at the visual jokes,

including a surreal stool by René Magritte and a coffee table by none other than Salvador Dalí.

Garden Court Hotel
520 Cowper St, Palo Alto ▪ (650) 322-9000 ▪ www. gardencourt.com ▪ Dis. access ▪ $$
The elegant, airy rooms in this Spanish-style hotel in downtown Palo Alto feature private terraces and marble bathrooms. Some rooms also have fireplaces.

Hotel des Arts
MAP G2 ▪ 447 Bush St ▪ (415) 956-3232 ▪ www.sfhoteldesarts.com ▪ $$
This art-themed hotel features clean, modern design, guest rooms designed by local artists, and a gallery presenting the work of international as well as local artists.

Hotel Monaco
MAP P3 ▪ 501 Geary St ▪ (415) 292-0100 ▪ www. monaco-sf.com ▪ Dis. access ▪ $$
Situated in the heart of the Theater District, this quirky but extremely comfortable hotel is run to perfection. The fairy-tale decor is joyously original, being at once a celebration of color and elegance, and the beds may be the most comfortable in the world. The stylish restaurant is an attraction in itself.

Hotel Rex
MAP P3 ▪ 562 Sutter St ▪ (415) 433-4434 ▪ www. thehotelrex.com ▪ Dis. access ▪ $$
Steeped in the literary and artistic traditions of California, this great little hotel boasts an intellectual air and decor reminiscent of 1930s salon society. Still, the rooms have the latest touches, as well as writing desks for guests to pursue their own creativity. The hotel also hosts readings, art shows and live music in the on-site Library Bar, where literary-themed cocktails are served.

The Inn Above Tide
30 El Portal, Sausalito ▪ (415) 332-9535 ▪ www. innabovetide.com ▪ Dis. access ▪ $$
The only hotel built directly on the Bay. The views across the Bay from the private balconies in the guest rooms are stunning, and there is a serene ambience. This is a wonderful choice, convenient to the city via the Golden Gate Bridge or a ferry ride. Guests can borrow bicycles from the hotel free of charge.

Inn at the Presidio
MAP D2 ▪ 42 Moraga Ave ▪ (415) 800-7356 ▪ www. innatthepresidio.com ▪ Dis. access ▪ $$
Housed in a historic building in the heart of Presidio, close to fabulous restaurants and museums, this elegant hotel has beautifully appointed yet simple rooms.

Petite Auberge
MAP G3 ■ 863 Bush St
■ (415) 928-6000 ■
www.petiteaubergesf.com
■ $$
This French Provincial-
styled hotel is a member
of the Joie de Vivre hotel
group. The ambience
combines the luxurious
and the rustic, with brass
pans hung on the walls
and pillow-top mattresses
on the beds. As well as
the complimentary
breakfast buffet, there are
freshly baked cookies
every afternoon.

W
MAP Q5 ■ 181 3rd St ■
(415) 777-5300 ■
www.wsanfrancisco.com
■ Dis. access ■ $$
Talk about trendy in this
town, and all convers-
ations will inevitably lead
to the W hotel. The decor
is minimalist, but with
luxury touches
throughout. Rooms
feature flat-screen TVs
and iPod Shuffles. The
clientele that come here
for drinks are chic
trendsetters, too.

Hotel G
MAP P3 ■ 386 Geary St
■ (415) 986-2000 ■ www.
hotelgsanfrancisco.com
■ $$$
Stay next to Union Square
in sleekly designed rooms
decorated in stylish greys
and whites with wooden
touches. The 2014
renovation of this 1908
building preserved many
original features while
adding modern comforts
to rooms like free Wi-Fi,
Smart TVs, honor bars,
and Nespresso makers.
The hotel shop sells chic
clothing and objects for
those who want to bring a
piece of G home.

Hotel Kabuki
MAP F3 ■ 1625 Post St
■ (415) 922-3200 ■ www.
jdvhotels.com/hotel-
kabuki ■ $$$
Taste a bit of Asian-style
hospitality in this boutique
hotel, which offers guests
deep soaking tubs,
Japanese gardens and a
Zen-like ambience.

Hotel Zephyr
MAP K3 ■ 250 Beach St
■ (415) 617-6555 ■
www.hotelzephyrsf.com
■ Dis. access ■ $$$
A weird and wacky naval
theme (think Popeye) give
the lobby, guest rooms,
and suites a humorous
marine feel, matching the
Fisherman's Wharf
location of this large,
upscale but friendly hotel.

Taj Campton Place
MAP P4 ■ 340 Stockton
St ■ (415) 781-5555 ■
www.lhw.com ■ Dis.
access ■ $$$
A member of the Leading
Small Hotels of the World
and definitely one of San
Francisco's finest, this
place aims to provide
personal attention to
each of its guests.
Expect to find the best of
everything here. The
restaurant, serving
California Cuisine, also
enjoys national ranking.

Traditional Hotels

Hotel Nikko
MAP Q3 ■ 222 Mason St ■
(415) 394-1111 ■
www.hotelnikkosf.com ■
Dis. access ■ $$
High-tech and minimalist
white marble interiors
radiate modernity in this
Japanese-style environ-
ment. Its cool comfort
and tranquil luxury, with
touches such as silk wall-

paper, soothe the spirit
and free the mind. The
excellent Anzu restaurant
creates the same
peaceful atmosphere.

Hyatt Regency
MAP N6 ■ 5 Embarcadero
Center ■ (415) 788-1234
■ www.sanfrancisco
regency.hyatt.com ■
Dis. access ■ $$
The 15-story atrium lobby,
one of the largest in the
world, has long plants
trailing down, a waterfall,
and glass elevators.
This waterfront hotel
have been through a
major renovation,
completed in 2015.

JW Marriott Hotel
MAP P3 ■ 500 Post St ■
(415) 771-8600 ■ www.
jwmarriottunionsquare.
com ■ Dis. access ■ $$
It's all about location
at this large, elegant
hotel situated in Union
Square. Rooms have all
modern amenities and a
24-hour butler service.
Guests rave about the
pillow-top mattresses.
The service is top-notch
and the beautifully
furnished lounge areas in
the lobby are welcoming
and relaxing.

Le Méridien
MAP N5 ■ 333 Battery St
■ (415) 296-2900 ■ www.
starwoodhotels.com ■
Dis. access ■ $$
Sleek and sophisticated,
Le Méridien is an elegant
hotel, with many of the
rooms offering views over
the Bay. Its restaurant,
Park Grill, serves
American cuisine and
has a lovely patio for al
fresco dining. The terrace
is also a great place to
enjoy drinks. The service
is first-class.

Palace Hotel

MAP P5 ■ 2 New Montgomery St ■ (415) 512-1111 ■ www.sfpalace.com ■ Dis. access ■ $$

Dating from 1875, this historic landmark hotel emanates architectural splendor. The gorgeous Garden Court (where traditional afternoon tea is served) and the original Maxfield Parrish mural in the Pied Piper Lounge are national treasures. The rooms are wonderful, but many do not offer views.

Sir Francis Drake

MAP P4 ■ 450 Powell St ■ (415) 391-8719 ■ www.sirfrancisdrake.com ■ Dis. access ■ $$

This splendid Art Deco landmark is situated just a block away from Union Square. The doormen wear Beefeater costumes and the cable cars glide by constantly. All in all, it has a very festive and colorful feel to it, both in the private rooms and in the bistro and two bars.

The Westin St. Francis

MAP P4 ■ 335 Powell St ■ (415) 397-7000 ■ www.westin.com ■ Dis. access ■ $$

This grand San Francisco institution still shines in its public rooms, but it has become a tour-group mediocrity otherwise. Nonetheless, the views from the tower rooms are still phenomenal.

Four Seasons

MAP P4 ■ 757 Market St ■ (415) 633-3000 ■ www.fourseasons.com ■ Dis. access ■ $$$

Designed with the business expense-account traveler in mind, this place has every sort of business amenity, including two phone lines with a high-speed Internet connection in each room, and a well-run business center.

Loews Regency

MAP N5 ■ 222 Sansome St ■ (415) 276-9888 ■ www.loewshotels.com ■ Dis. access ■ $$$

Located on the top 11 floors of the third tallest building in Downtown, this is one of the classiest hotels you'll find in San Francisco. It offers splendid views over the Bay and city. It was formerly the Mandarin Oriental, but it is now run by Loews and in 2015 it re-emerged after renovations were made to its guest rooms, lobby, and restaurant.

Ritz-Carlton Resort

1 Miramontes Point Rd, Half Moon Bay ■ (650) 712-7000 ■ www.ritzcarlton.com ■ Dis. access ■ $$$

A rambling mansion set on its own verdant bluff, overlooking the Pacific, this is the perfect retreat from which to enjoy the Bay Area. The resort offers guests two golf courses.

Hilltop Hotels

Hotel Sausalito

16 El Portal at Bridgeway, Sausalito ■ (415) 332-0700 ■ www.hotelsausalito.com ■ Dis. access ■ $

With a quirky back story, this inviting boutique hotel has luxurious rooms and suites decorated in pastel hues that offer park and harbor views.

Queen Anne

MAP F3 ■ 1590 Sutter at Octavia ■ (415) 441-2828 ■ www.queenanne.com ■ Dis. access ■ $

Built in 1890, this old mansion has been lovingly refurbished according to Victorian taste. The rooms are individually decorated and filled with antiques. The continental breakfast is complimentary, and your morning newspaper, too.

Claremont Hotel Club and Spa

41 Tunnel Rd, Berkeley ■ (510) 843-3000 ■ www.claremontresort.com ■ Dis. access ■ $$

This country club-style resort in the Berkeley Hills was built in 1915 and still retains the feel of that era. There are business services, a fitness center, two pools, tennis courts, and views of the Golden Gate Bridge.

Fairmont

MAP N3 ■ 950 Mason St ■ (415) 772-5000 ■ www.fairmont.com ■ Dis. access ■ $$

"Opulent" and "palatial" barely begin to describe this *grande dame* of San Francisco's hotels, taking pride of place on Nob Hill. The rooms and service are commensurate with its superior status.

Hotel Drisco

MAP E2 ■ 2901 Pacific Ave ■ (415) 346-2880 ■ www.hoteldrisco.com ■ Dis. access ■ $$

This Pacific Heights property is one of the Leading Small Hotels of the World, and, although the elegance is perhaps a little too understated, it delivers on service.

Details include complimentary continental breakfast and morning newspaper, as well as some of the very best vistas San Francisco has to offer.

InterContinental Mark Hopkins
MAP N3 ■ 1 Nob Hill ■ (415) 392-3434 ■ www.intercontinentalmarkhopkins.com ■ Dis. access ■ $$
The Top of the Mark restaurant is, of course, a major pull, with its 360-degree panoramic views of the city, and the service is genuinely caring. The rooms are provided with every amenity and achieve an excellent standard of comfort.

Laurel Inn
MAP E3 ■ 444 Presidio Ave ■ (415) 567-8467 ■ www.jdvhotels.com ■ Dis. access ■ $$
This stylish hotel is located in Presidio Heights, and is decorated in a hip mid-century fashion. Some rooms feature kitchenettes, and they all come with flat-screen TVs and Blu-Ray players. Breakfast is included and there is also free parking.

The Scarlet Huntington
MAP N3 ■ 1075 California St ■ (415) 474-5400 ■ www.thescarlethotels.com ■ $$
Situated at the top of Nob Hill, across from Grace Cathedral, this hotel feels like the clubby apartment of a rich uncle with impeccable taste. The rooms are luxurious and there's an excellent

restaurant, plus a spa where you can get a champagne facial.

Stanford Court Renaissance
MAP N3 ■ 905 California St ■ (415) 989-3500 ■ www.stanfordcourt.com ■ $$
Long a business favorite, this hotel is situated near the top of Nob Hill, handy to everything Downtown. The stained-glass dome in the lobby gives it a grand feel. There are marble baths and canopy beds in some rooms.

The Ritz-Carlton
MAP N4 ■ 600 Stockton St ■ (415) 296-7465 ■ www.ritzcarlton.com ■ Dis. access ■ $$$
If you want to experience the ultimate in luxury and thoughtful service, this is the place. Views from the perfectly appointed rooms are magnificent, the staff are at the top of their game, and the food is nothing short of sublime.

Gay and Lesbian Hotels

Bel Abri
837 California Blvd, Napa ■ (707) 253-2100 ■ www.belabri.net ■ Dis. access ■ $
Rooms in this Wine Country inn have shutters, French tapestries, and wrought-iron features. Most rooms also include a fireplace, and two of them have Jacuzzis.

Chateau Tivoli
MAP E3 ■ 1057 Steiner St ■ (415) 776-5462 ■ www.chateautivoli.com ■ No air conditioning ■ $
Rooms and suites in this stunning old building

are named after Mark Twain, Enrico Caruso, Jack London, and others, to remind guests of San Francisco's illustrious history in the arts. Rooms are furnished with four-poster beds and feature fireplaces and bay windows.

Inn on Castro
MAP E5 ■ 321 Castro St ■ (415) 861-0321 ■ www.innoncastro.com ■ No air conditioning ■ Dis. access ■ $
The very friendly owner of this B&B seems to have thought of everything to make your stay in the heart of the Castro as pleasurable as possible. He's always ready with maps and advice on where to go. Comfort is key, in bright rooms filled with art and plants.

The Inn San Francisco
MAP F5 ■ 943 South Van Ness St ■ (415) 641-0188 ■ www.innsf.com ■ No air conditioning ■ $
This fine Victorian mansion serves a buffet breakfast in charming parlors. The garden has a redwood hot tub, plus a sundeck with a panoramic view of the city.

Meadowlark Country House
601 Petrified Forest Rd, Calistoga ■ (707) 942-5651 ■ www.meadowlarkinn.com ■ No air conditioning ■ $
In the heart of the Wine Country, this elegant guesthouse is situated on an estate with great facilities such as a mineral water hot tub and heated pool, and a Finnish dry sauna.

For a key to hotel price categories see p142

The Parker Guest House

MAP F5 ▪ 520 Church St ▪ (415) 621-3222 ▪ www.parkerguesthouse.com ▪ No air conditioning ▪ $
An Edwardian mini-mansion, located just steps away from various gay bars and restaurants, this guesthouse has expansive gardens and sun decks.

The Willows Inn

MAP E4 ▪ 710 14th St ▪ (415) 431-4770 ▪ www.willowssf.com ▪ No en-suite bathrooms ▪ No air conditioning ▪ $
This restored Edwardian house is conveniently located close to public transport links in the gay Castro District. The interior decor is a blend of handcrafted willow furnishings, antique dressers, and cozy comforters. Kimono-style bathrobes are also provided.

Beck's Motor Lodge

MAP F4 ▪ 2222 Market St ▪ (415) 621-8212 ▪ www.becksmotorlodge.com ▪ $$
Basic but nicely updated rooms are on offer in this no-smoking lodge with a private sun deck, as well as free parking and Wi-Fi. Situated in a lively area of the city, it is popular with gay men.

Castro Suites

MAP E4 ▪ 927 14th St ▪ (415) 437-1783 ▪ www.castrosuites.com ▪ No air conditioning ▪ Dis. access ▪ $$
This restored 1890s Italianate Victorian mansion has great views of Downtown and the Bay. With a minimum 30-day stay, accommodations are decorated with a mixture of original art, contemporary furniture, and plants. The kitchen comes equipped with a dishwasher, washing machine, and microwave.

Neighborhood Hotels

Hotel Del Sol

MAP E2 ▪ 3100 Webster St ▪ (415) 921-5520 ▪ www.thehoteldelsol.com ▪ No air conditioning ▪ $
Described as "festive and spacious," this boutique hotel really is a ray of sunshine. Bright colors and cheerful patterns greet you around every corner, and the staff is just as nice as can be. This is an especially great place to stay if you are traveling with kids.

Marina Motel

MAP E2 ▪ 2576 Lombard St ▪ (415) 921-9406 ▪ www.marinamotel.com ▪ $
Tucked away in a flower-filled Mediterranean courtyard decorated with murals, this motel offers guests a peaceful oasis right in the heart of the beautiful Marina District, close to restaurants and public transport links. Rooms are simple and clean, and parking is included.

Pacific Heights Inn

MAP F2 ▪ 1555 Union St ▪ (415) 776-3310 ▪ www.pacificheightsinn.com ▪ No air conditioning ▪ $
Situated on a quiet block close to public transport links, this motel offers basic but comfortable rooms. There is free on-site parking, Wi-Fi, and a continental breakfast. Some rooms also feature kitchens.

Phoenix Hotel

MAP Q2 ▪ 601 Eddy St ▪ (415) 776-1380 ▪ www.jdvhotels.com ▪ Dis. access ▪ $
Johnny Depp, REM band members, and the late John F. Kennedy, Jr have all stayed in this retro-style motorlodge with a courtyard pool, but it's located a bit too close to the gritty Tenderloin area for all but the most self-assured. Continental breakfast is included, and the popular restaurant/bar attracts hipsters from all across the city.

Seal Rock Inn

MAP A3 ▪ 545 Point Lobos Ave ▪ (415) 752-8000 ▪ www.sealrockinn.com ▪ $
In a handy location for visiting Cliff House and Land's End (see p117), as well as the Palace of the Legion of Honor. Rooms are large, though plain, and there's a sun deck, table tennis and outdoor pool for the summer months. Free parking is available.

Stanyan Park Hotel

MAP D4 ▪ 750 Stanyan St ▪ (415) 751-1000 ▪ www.stanyanpark.com ▪ No air conditioning ▪ Dis. access ▪ $
Listed on the National Register of Historic Places, this Victorian hotel has been receiving guests since 1904. It is located right on Golden Gate Park and is decorated in period style. Continental breakfast and free Wi-Fi is included.

The Tuscan
MAP K3 ▪ 425 North
Point St ▪ (415) 561-1100
▪ www.tuscanhotel.com
▪ Dis. access ▪ $
Although it's part of the
Best Western chain, don't
let that put you off as this
is one of the stylish
branches. It is located
right in the heart of
Fisherman's Wharf, and
staying here takes some
of the touristy edge off the
neighborhood. Features
include a mirrored wall in
every room, and free
coffee and tea.

Twin Peaks Hotel
MAP F4 ▪ 2160 Market St
▪ (415) 863-2909 ▪ Some
en-suite bathrooms ▪ No
air conditioning ▪ $
Clean, quiet and comfort-
able, but it doesn't get any
more straightforward
than this. The advantage
here is the location – in
close proximity to the
Castro, Hayes Valley, and
the Mission.

Jackson Court
MAP F2 ▪ 2198 Jackson
St ▪ (415) 929-7670 ▪
www.jacksoncourt.com
▪ $$
Located in the Pacific
Heights area, this is a
magnificent 1900
brownstone mansion.
The wood-paneled parlor
is an inviting place, and the
stone fireplace provides a
warm glow in which to
enjoy afternoon tea.

Pier 2620
MAP K3 ▪ 2620 Jones St ▪
(415) 268-5925 ▪ www.
pier2620hotel.com ▪ $$
Located in the buzzing
Fisherman's Wharf area,
a short walk from Pier 39,
and with lots of shops and
restaurants on the
surrounding streets, this

hotel, renovated in 2015,
offers 233 comfortable
rooms. Street noise can
be an issue, so ask for a
room facing the courtyard
if you are a light sleeper.

B&Bs and Guesthouses

Cliff Crest Inn B&B
407 Cliff St, Santa Cruz ▪
(831) 427-2609 ▪ www.
cliffcrestinn.com ▪ No
air conditioning ▪
Dis. access ▪ $
Surrounded by redwoods,
the rooms in this Queen
Anne Victorian are graced
with fresh flowers, and
some also have views
over the Bay.

Hayes Valley Inn
MAP F3 ▪ 417 Gough St ▪
(415) 431-9131 ▪ www.
hayesvalleyinn.com ▪ $
A budget B&B option,
but with a certain charm.
The basic rooms have
shared bathrooms.

Panama Hotel
4 Bayview St, San Rafael
▪ (415) 457-3993 ▪ www.
panamahotel.com ▪ No
air conditioning ▪ $
This friendly, eccentric
place is filled with eclectic
period touches. Rooms
have names such as the
Bordello Room and the
Captain's Cabin – each
with its own tale to tell.
Pets are welcome.

The Red Victorian
MAP E4 ▪ 1665 Haight St
▪ (415) 864-1978 ▪ www.
redvic.com ▪ No air
conditioning ▪ $
A hostel inspired by
hippie ideals, here, every
morning, you meet the
owners and other guests
to engage in intelligent
conversation around the
breakfast table at the

"Peace Café." Each guest
room is also designed to
celebrate love.

Sleep Over Sauce
MAP F4 ▪ 135 Gough St ▪
(415) 621-0896 ▪ www.
sleepsf.com ▪ No air
conditioning ▪ Dis. access
▪ $
This boutique guesthouse
is a great find in the
bustle of the city. The
eight rooms are clean,
modern, and comfortable.
Its restaurant, Sauce, is
award-winning.

White Swan Inn
MAP N3 ▪ 845 Bush St ▪
(415) 775-1755 ▪ www.
whiteswaninnsf.com ▪ $
This quaint B&B is like a
country inn in the heart of
Downtown, with bright
floral prints, Victorian-
style canopied beds, and
cozy fireplaces. An
evening wine reception
and English breakfast are
both complimentary.

Cavallo Point Lodge
601 Murray Circle, Fort
Baker, Sausalito ▪
(415) 339-4700 ▪ www.
cavallopoint.com ▪
Dis. access ▪ No air
conditioning ▪ $$
A former military base,
this luxury lodge has the
charm of a B&B and is
set in beautiful
surroundings at the foot
of the Golden Gate
Bridge. Rooms are
comfortable and spacious.

Golden Gate Hotel
MAP B4 ▪ 775 Bush
St, 94108 ▪ (415) 392-
3702 ▪ www.goldengate
hotel.com ▪ $$
Tea and freshly baked
cookies are available
every afternoon in this
family-run hotel with
small, luxurious rooms.

For a key to hotel price categories see p142

Mountain Home Inn
810 Panoramic Hwy, Mill Valley ■ (415) 381-9000 ■ www.mtnhomeinn.com ■ Dis. access ■ $$
Step out of the door of this quaint mountainside inn and be blown away by the spectacular views it has of San Francisco Bay and Mount Tamalpais. Situated just 20 minutes from Downtown, this hikers' paradise invites you to meander to the beachside town of Stinson or to historic Muir Woods. Afterward, indulge in hearty gourmet meals.

The Pelican Inn
10 Pacific Way, Muir Beach ■ (415) 383-6000 ■ www.pelicaninn.com ■ No air conditioning ■ $$
Majestically positioned deep in a valley, each of the seven rooms has antiques, and a roaring fire is lit every day in the inglenook fireplace.

The Union Street Inn
MAP E2 ■ 2229 Union St ■ (415) 346-0424 ■ www.unionstreetinn.com ■ $$
Combining the elegance and gentility of an Edwardian home, located just up from the Marina and right on fashionable Union Street. The individually decorated rooms are all spacious, with original antiques and art, fine linens, fresh flowers, and compliment-ary chocolates and fruit.

Hotel Vitale
MAP H2 ■ 8 Mission St ■ (415) 278-3700 ■ www.hotelvitale.com ■ Dis. access ■ $$$
The amenities reign supreme at this urban oasis looming above the city's spectacular water-front. Check out your preferred style of pillow in the pillow library, attend a complimentary morning yoga class, relax in one of the outdoor rooftop soaking tubs, or enjoy luxury spa services.

Budget Hotels

Coventry Motor Inn
MAP F2 ■ 1901 Lombard St ■ (415) 567-1200 ■ www.coventrymotorinn.com ■ Dis. access ■ $
A good, basic motel, offering large, pleasant rooms with bay windows, located on the Marina's "Motel Row." It isn't beautiful, but it's functional and reliable. All rooms are no-smoking, and parking is complimentary. A minimum stay may apply on some weekends.

Cow Hollow Motor Inn and Suites
MAP E2 ■ 2190 Lombard St ■ (415) 921-5800 ■ www.cowhollowmotorinn.com ■ Dis. access ■ $
Larger-than-average rooms, with floral wallpaper and traditional furniture giving them a homey feel. Some suites have Oriental carpets accenting wood floors, marble fireplaces, and antiques. There is free parking, and it is a no-smoking hotel.

The Good Hotel
MAP R3 ■ 112 7th St ■ (415) 621-7001 ■ www.thegoodhotel.com ■ No air conditioning ■ $
The Good Hotel promises a stylish, sustainable stay at a great price. Although the rooms may be on the small side, they come with iPod docking stations, free Wi-Fi, and decor that is modern and clean. Bicycles are also available for guest use.

Hostelling International Downtown
MAP P3 ■ 312 Mason St ■ (415) 788-5604 ■ www.sfhostels.org ■ No en-suite bathrooms ■ No air conditioning ■ $
This location is Action Central for all the major sights. Rooms hold up to five beds. All major public transportation is just outside and there's lots of tourist information available, too.

Hostelling International Fisherman's Wharf
MAP F1 ■ Fort Mason, Building 240 ■ (415) 771-7277 ■ www.sfhostels.org ■ Dis. access ■ $
This hostel offers free breakfast, Wi-Fi, and parking. It's just a short walk to everything along the Bayshore.

Inn on Broadway
MAP E3 ■ 2201 Van Ness Ave ■ (415) 776-7900 ■ www.broadwaymanor.com ■ $
All rooms at this no-smoking inn feature flat-screen TVs, and coffee- and tea-making facilities. Free parking and Wi-Fi.

Marin Headlands Hostel
Fort Barry, Building 941, Field & Bunker Rds ■ (415) 331-2777 ■ www.norcalhostels.org ■ No en-suite bathrooms ■ No air conditioning ■ $
Dorms and private rooms, some for families, near Muir Woods and beaches.

Marina Inn
MAP F2 ▪ 3110 Octavia St at Lombard ▪ (415) 928-1000 ▪ www.marinainn.com ▪ No air conditioning ▪ Dis. access ▪ $
The charm of a San Francisco Victorian awaits you here. The marble lobby is the focal point of this four-story hotel built in 1924, and the sitting room is the setting for its continental breakfasts. But the real draws are the price and the location, which can't be beat.

The Mosser
MAP Q4 ▪ 54 4th St ▪ (415) 986-4400 ▪ www.themosser.com ▪ No air conditioning ▪ $
It's hard to beat this location, less than a block from the center of Market Street and the nearest subway station. The Mosser has a few other things going for it as well, namely clean, Ikea-furnished rooms, great prices, and a terrific bistro off its lobby.

San Francisco Zen Center
MAP F4 ▪ 300 Page St ▪ (415) 863-3136 ▪ www.sfzc.org ▪ Dis. access ▪ No en-suite bathrooms ▪ No air conditioning ▪ $
The Zen Center has several comfortable, quiet rooms available for those who are interested in learning more about Zen practices.

San Remo
MAP K3 ▪ 2237 Mason St ▪ (415) 776-8688 ▪ www.sanremohotel.com ▪ No en-suite bathrooms ▪ No air conditioning ▪ $
North Beach's biggest bargain is full of charms. Each room is decorated with antiques, and the corridors feature brass railings and hanging plants under skylights. Every room has its own sink, while the other bathroom facilities are down the hall.

The Cartwright Hotel
MAP B4 ▪ 524 Sutter St, 94102 ▪ (415) 421-2865 ▪ www.cartwrightunionsquare.com ▪ $$
This pet-friendly hotel has a fireplace in the lobby, simple rooms, and free Wi-Fi. It also has a great location, near the Theater District.

Apartments and Private Homes

The Gateway
MAP N6 ▪ 460 Davis Court ▪ (888) 220-0301 ▪ www.thegateway.com ▪ Dis. access ▪ $
Location is everything at these fully furnished, extended-stay apartments, which are just steps away from a host of retail stores, restaurants, and local transportation options. Offering every amenity and service one could possibly want when planning a long visit, these apartments promise a convenient and comfortable stay.

The Monroe Hotel
MAP N1 ▪ 1870 Sacramento St ▪ (415) 474-6200 ▪ www.monroeresidenceclub.com ▪ No air conditioning ▪ Dis. access ▪ $
Amid the mansions of Pacific Heights, the Monroe combines the best elements of a hotel and an apartment. American-style breakfasts and four-course dinners are included. Maid service is also provided.

Pinnacle Suites
MAP N3 ▪ 899 Pine St ▪ (415) 421-1899 ▪ www.thepinnacleatnobhill.com ▪ Dis. access ▪ $
This all-suite hotel is perched on top of Nob Hill. The suites feature kitchens equipped with refrigerators and microwaves. There are housekeeping and laundry services, voicemail, cable TV, and a valet service (small fee).

Casa Luna
MAP E5 ▪ 4058 17th St between Market & Castro ▪ (415) 738-8121 ▪ www.casalunasf.com ▪ No air conditioning ▪ Dis. access ▪ $$
This restored Edwardian building has been converted into two luxury apartments in the heart of the Castro district. It boasts eco-friendly, stylish furnishings, Egyptian cotton sheets, and Jacuzzi soaking tubs. Each apartment has two bedrooms and two full baths and is in a very safe and convenient location.

Oakwood Pine Street
MAP N6 ▪ 1 Pine St at Market ▪ (877) 902-0832 ▪ No air conditioning ▪ www.oakwood.com ▪ $$
With a minimum stay of 30 days and starting prices lower than most hotels, these apartments offer one- and two-bedroom options, all with private balconies and fully equipped kitchens. Many have views of the Bay Bridge and the Financial District. The location is great, too.

General Index

Acknowledgments

Author
Native San Franciscan Jeffrey Kennedy now lives mainly in Italy and Spain. A graduate of Stanford University, he spends his time producing, writing, and acting. He is also co-author of *Top 10 Rome* and author of *Top 10 Mallorca* and *Top 10 Miami & The Keys*.

Additional Contributor Karen Misuraca

Publishing Director Georgina Dee

Publisher Vivien Antwi

Design Director Phil Ormerod

Editorial Michelle Crane, Rachel Fox, Fíodhna Ní Ghríofa, Freddie Marriage, Sally Schafer, Scarlett O'Hara, Anna Streiffert, Christine Stroyan

Design Richard Czapnik, Fatima Jamadar

Picture Research Phoebe Lowndes, Susie Peachey, Ellen Root, Oran Tarjan

Cartography Uma Bhattacharya, Simonetta Giori, Suresh Kumar, Casper Morris, James Macdonald, Reetu Pandey

DTP Jason Little, George Nimmo, Joanna Stenlake

Production Olivia Jeffries

Factchecker Lauren Viera

Proofreader Sam Cook

Indexer Hilary Bird

Illustrator chrisorr.com

First edition created by Sargasso Media Ltd, London

Commissioned Photography
Christopher P Baker, Peter Anderson, Lee Foster, Robert Holmes, Neil Lukas, Andrew McKinney, Susanna Price, Rough Guides/Nelson Hancock, Rough Guides/Martin Richardson, Rough Guides/ Paul Whitfield, Robert Vente.

Picture Credits

The publisher would like to thank the following for their kind permission to reproduce their photographs:

(**Key:** a-above; b-below/bottom; c-center; f-far; l-left; r-right; t-top)

4Corners: SIME/Maurizio Rellini 14-5c; Susanne Kremer 120-1.

Absinthe Brasserie & Bar: Postcard PR 107tr.

Alamy Images: Mark Bassett 50tl; Jan Butchofsky 25cra; Danita Delimont 62t; Design Pics Inc/Laura Ciapponi 27b; Randy Duchaine 18cr; Dianne Feinstein statue by Lisa Reinertson 43bl; Enlightened Images/Gary Crabbe 119cl; Seth Grant 14bl; Michael Halberstadt 104bl; Dave G. Houser 63cla; Bob Kreisel 61cra, 67tr; Jackie Link 46bc; Stefano Politi Markovina 4crb; Mountain Light/ Galen Rowell 12br; Eric Nathan 23clb; Nikreates 68t, 69cl, 80t; North Wind Picture Archives 42bl; William Perry 35bl; PhotoBliss 116tl; The Print

Collector 42t; Robert Rosenblum 26bl; Leonid Serebrennikov 92br; Stars and Stripes 64b; ZUMA Press, Inc 27tr.

Asian Art Museum: Orange Photography 52b.

AWL Images: Stefano Politi Markovina 4t.

Blue Bottle Cafe: Claypix.com/Clay McLachlan 76bl.

California Academy of Sciences: Tim Griffith 26tl; Chris Picon 26-7c.

Cartoon Art Museum: 55tl.

Cliff House: 75tr.

Le Colonial: Le Colonial 71tr.

Courtesy of the Contemporary Jewish Museum, San Francisco.: Bruce Damonte 33tr.

Corbis: Atlantide Phototravel/Massimo Borchi 30b; Morton Beebe 23tl; Bettmann 21tr; Gerald French 90-1; Historical 47tr; Johannes Mann 1; Masterfile/ Jose Luis Stephens 32tl; Proehl Studios/Steve Proehl 2tl, 8-9, Mural in the Beach Chalet at Ocean Beach by artist, Lucien Labaudt 51br; San Francisco Chronicle 13tl; Phil Schermeister 49tr; Marco Simoni 3tl, 84-5; Sunset Boulevard 20crb; Captain W. Swasey 88cla; Wonwoo Lee 15br;

de Young Museum: 29bl; Gregory Bertolini 28-9c; Painting of Boatmen on the Missouri George Caleb Bingham 29tl; Henrik Kam 28cla; Michael Layefsky 11ca.

Delfina Restaurant: Eric Wolfinger 115b.

Dorling Kindersley Ltd: Courtesy of Grace Cathedral 87br; Jack London statue by Cedric Wentworth 44c; Willie Mays statue by William Behrends at AT&T Park 109tc; Courtesy of the Natural History Museum, London/Tim Parmenter 128cb.

Dreamstime.com: Andreykr 22-3c, 78tl; Blackkango 110-1t; Brandon Bourdages 82cla; Bpperry 11br; Canbalci 10-1t; Chee-onn Leong 59t; Cminor 58b; Kobby Dagan 82br; Drserg 53cr; Efaah0 17cr; F8grapher 19cr; Filiola 11tr; Friday 129cra; Gmargittai 25bc; Hivola 60tl; Issalina 12bl; Jabiru 18ca; Jerryway 16-7c, 62cr; Jetjock 24-5c; Jewhyte 11cr; Jiawangkun 88cb; Jpldesigns 48tl; Kazmaniac 36-7c; Luckydoor 96tl; Lunamarina 7br, 103t; Lyngbyvej 19cl; Maciejbledowski 18-9b; Martinimolcan 12-3c, 110bl; Andres Garcia Martin 57t; Masterlu 109br; Meinzahm 17clb; Eli Mordechai 60bl; Luciano Mortula 57cl; William Perry 48br; Photoquest 24bl, 56bl; Povalec 10bc; Qweszxcj 6tr; Radekdrewek 16clb; Radkol 83tl; Rahurlburt 34cl; Ralfweber 4cra; Rfoxphoto 34bc; Robynmac 77tr; Sborisov 3tr, 10cl, 132-3; Sf_smk 4bl; Spvvkr 126t; Srongkrod 80br; Tasstock 104tr; Pamela Tekiel 18clb; Rudy Umans 32t; Unfetteredmind 125t; Ventdusud 105cl; Vonshots 4cla; Walleyelj 4br, 16br; Wizreist 18tr; Wolterk 97t; Zhukovsky Sphinx statue by Arthur Putnam 28c, 36bl.

elizabethW: 100br.

Exploratorium, www.exploratorium.edu: Gayle Laird 67clb.

The Fairmont, San Francisco: 70t.

The Fairmont Sonoma Mission Inn & Spa: 38cl.

Fillmore Street Jazz Festival: anupma/Denise Lamott Public Relations 83tr.

Courtesy of Fraenkel Gallery, San Francisco: 54bl.

Gayle's Bakery: Gayle's Bakery 131tr.

Getty Images: Richard Cummins 66t; De Agostini Picture Library 108tl; Rick Gerharter 130; Glow Images, Inc 86tl; Hoffmann Photography 4clb; Hulton Archive 43tr; Izzet Keribar 94t; The LIFE Picture Collection/Ralph Crane 21bl; Lonely Planet 113tr; Tim Mosenfelder 81tr; Movie Poster Image Art 13cb; Radius Images 118b; Redferns/Daniel Boczarski 45cl, /RB 45tr; Ezra Shaw 61tr; Sports Studio Photos 45bl; The Washington Post/John Cohen 44tl; WIN-Initiative Labyrinth artwork by Eduardo Aguilera formed of rocks overlooking ocean 117b; www.35mmNegative.com 98t; Barry Winiker 15tl.

Harry Denton's Starlight Room: Kimpton Group 70br.

The Hess Collection: 11crb, 37cr.

Marmalade: Marmalade 106tl.

Meritage Resort and Spa: Rex Gelert 39cla.

Midnight Sun: 73tr.

Moscone Center: SMG/SFCF/John Louie 33bl.

Oakland Museum of California: 128cla.

Outerlands: Eric Wolfinger 123tr.

Paul's Hat Works: 122bl.

Paxton Gate: Jessica Watson 112br.

Powell's Sweet Shoppe: 130c.

Quince: 95ca; Patrik Argast 74t.

Rex Features: 20tl; Hans Kwiotek 78br.

Robert Harding Picture Library: Richard Cummins 34-5c, 99cl; Juergen Richter 36cl; P. Schickert 2tr, 40-1; Marco Simoni 22bl.

San Francisco Museum Of Modern Art: Michael Jackson and Bubbles © Jeff Koons 31bc; Henrik Kam 30tr.

Schein & Schein: 93tl.

Silverado Resort and Spa: Joann Dost 39b.

Smuggler's Cove: Allison Webber 77bl.

Spruce: 75bl.

St. John Coltrane African Orthodox Church: 49cla.

Tacolicious: Aubrie Pick 101tr.

Tartine Bakery & Cafe: OpenKitchenPhotography/ Eric Wolfinger 76tr.

Trick Dog: Allison Webber Photography 114tr

Jacket

Front and spine – **Robert Harding Picture Library:** P. Schickert.
Back – **AWL Images:** Danita Delimont Stock t.

Pull out map cover

Robert Harding Picture Library: P. Schickert.

All other images are: © Dorling Kindersley. For further information see www.dkimages.com.

*As a guide to abbreviations in visitor information blocks: **Adm** = admission charge; **Dis. Access** = disabled access; **D** = dinner; **L** = lunch.*

DK | Penguin Random House

Printed and bound in China

First American Edition, 2003
Published in the United States by
DK Publishing, 345 Hudson Street,
New York, New York 10014

Copyright 2003, 2016 © Dorling
Kindersley Limited

A Penguin Random House Company

15 16 17 18 10 9 8 7 6 5 4 3 2 1

**Reprinted with revisions 2004, 2006,
2007, 2008, 2009, 2010, 2011, 2012,
2013, 2014, 2016**

Published in Great Britain by Dorling
Kindersley Limited.

A catalog record for this book is available
from the Library of Congress.

ISSN 1479-344X
ISBN 978-1-4654-4091-4

MIX
Paper from
responsible sources
FSC™ C018179

Street Index